REALIZATIONS

PERSONAL EMPOWERMENT THROUGH SELF-AWARENESS

by
William A. Guillory

Innovations Publishing, Salt Lake City, Utah

Reprint of the quotes by J. Krishnamurti from *The Awakening of Intelligence* is gratefully acknowledged by permission from the Krishnamurti Foundation of America, Ojai, CA.

Quotes by Sheldon Kopp are reprinted by permission of the author and publisher; Science and Behavior Books, 1972, Palo Alto, CA.

First Printing, 1985
Second Printing, 1987
Third Printing, 1990

Book design: Scott Engen, Salt Lake City, Utah

Copyright © 1984 by William A. Guillory

Library of Congress Catalog Card Number: 85-60283

ISBN (softcover): ISBN: 0-933241-00-3

Printed in the United States of America.

Comments or requests for information may be forwarded to:

Innovations Consulting, Inc.
488 East 6400 South
Suite 475
Salt Lake City, Utah 84107
(801) 268-3313

To Danny

A human being is a part of the whole, called by us the "Universe," a part limited in time and space. He experiences himself, his thoughts, and feelings as something separated from the rest — a kind of optical delusion of his consciousness. This delusion is a kind of prison for us, restricting us to our personal desires and to affection for a few persons nearest to us. Our task must be to free ourselves from this prison by widening our circle of compassion to embrace all living creatures and the whole of nature in its beauty.

Albert Einstein

CONTENTS

ACKNOWLEDGMENTS *ix*

PREFACE *xi*

1. THE FIRST STEP TO CHANGE IS AWARENESS 1
Would You Like to Go Backpacking?
Aware and Aware/Unaware
If I Am Unaware That I Am Unaware, Then I'm Lost

2. REALIZATIONS 9
What Is a Realization?
Fear
Sharing Realizations
Are Realizations Logical?
Realizations Are Not Intellectual

3. IS SURVIVAL THE DRIVING FORCE? 17
Survival Is Innate
Early Life Decisions
The Evolution of a Reality

4. RESPONSIBILITY IS SYNONYMOUS WITH OWNERSHIP 23
What Is Responsibility?
Ego As a Barrier to Responsibility
Levels of Responsibility

5. DISTINGUISHING EXPERIENCE FROM INTERPRETATION 31
Introduction
It's a Matter of Distinction
Have We Been Making This Distinction?
Being Natural and Being Normal
Being Natural Comes Without Effort

6. KNOWLEDGE AND REALITY   **43**
> How Do I Know What I Know?
> Fundamental Life Principle
> Construction of a Reality

7. RELATIONSHIP   **53**
> How We Put It Together
> Show Me the Way Out
> Qualities of a Relationship That Works
> An Exercise or Two
> What's the Message?

8. PROBLEMS AND RELATED STRESS, AND RESOLUTIONS   **63**
> The True Source of Problems Can Be Deceptive
> What Is a Problem?
> Analysis of a Problem
> What's the Connection Between Upsetting Problems and Stress?
> Stress Management Through Problem Resolution

9. COMMUNICATION WITH INTENT   **77**
> What Was That I Said?
> Subliminal Communication
> It's About Where We're Coming From!
> I Never Thought About Gossip in That Way!
> Does Accepting Others Have Anything to Do with Me?
> Communication with Intent

10. FOR THOSE WHO CHASE STARS   **91**
> What's a Star-Chaser?
> So Where's the Pay-Off, If Any?
> What's Required to Be a "Star-Chaser?"
> On Being Creative
> Personal Freedom, an Essential Requirement for Creativity
> Star-Chasing and Risking Are Really One and the Same

ACKNOWLEDGMENTS

I would like to acknowledge the Centers Network, San Francisco, California, for providing me the initial opportunity to discover an expanded quality of living. The Network's programs and the writings of J. Krishnamurti have had the major impact on my most recent experience of living and, correspondingly, on my integrated thinking expressed in this book. I would like to thank those who have made significant contributions to the development of the workshops: Susan, Layne, Herb and Linda. I am indebted to the innumerable individuals who contributed to my personal growth and education, particularly Brian Regnier, and to those who have participated in my workshops. I am thankful for the assistance of Ms. Cindy J. Clark at the University of Utah for her contribution in typing the manuscript and for Ms. Cordelle Yoder at the University of California, Berkeley, who also assisted in the typing. I am finally thankful to Anne who was a constant source of encouragement and inspiration.

PREFACE

This book is written with the intent that it serve as a source of new awareness in our personal and professional lives; that it might serve as a seed or a catalyst in having us reexamine our beliefs, assumptions, and presuppositions about the way we experience living. At a more fundamental level, it is intended to provoke a new way of *seeing* ourselves with respect to relationships that I refer to as *an altered way of being*. This altered way of being comes about spontaneously and from within and does not involve beliefs, dogma, or an expected mode of behavior. It simply requires the open-mindedness and the willingness to become aware, as a prerequisite, to fundamentally changing counterproductive aspects of our behavior that we act out unconsciously.

This book is also intended to communicate a sense of the approach used in our workshop presentations to organizations, both in the public and private sectors, as well as to special heterogeneous and homogeneous groups.

Much of the material used in this book is the result of fundamental and permanent changes which I have undergone as a result of *realizations* derived from my own personal experiences. As a result, many of the shared examples will be about these experiences. Therefore, it is my intent that any new awareness that you have will lead ultimately to realizations that are of fundamental importance in your life.

William A. Guillory
April, 1985

The most significant feedback we have received since distributing the first printing of REALIZATIONS is that the book is "timeless." In fact, every time I reread this book, I discover some new insight occurring in my life at that time. Since the book is a gift to me in terms of my having the opportunity to write it, I am privileged to share this gift with you.

William A. Guillory
June, 1987

As we do the third printing, I am gratified by the number of people who write to let me know how much they value this book. I am pleased that my shared experiences of continuing growth are providing a similar process for others, both personally and professionally.

William A. Guillory
October, 1990

Chapter One

THE FIRST STEP TO CHANGE IS AWARENESS

*"If I am at least aware
That I am unaware that
I am unaware of something,
Then I am not totally lost."*

The Author

Would You Like to Go Backpacking?

I remember the first time I went on a backpacking trip. It was shortly after I had moved to Utah to live. It was a twelve-mile hike in the Wind River Mountain Range of Wyoming. My filled backpack weighed about fifty pounds in addition to borrowed sleeping gear. I was ready!

I noticed that some of the group were "getting into shape" by walking up and down hills and exercising the week prior to the hike. I figured they were simply "aging prematurely" or not in as good shape as I obviously was. Nevertheless, I didn't want to seem too cocky, so I walked a couple of swift miles on flat terrain daily just to prove to myself that I could go out and hike twenty miles if it were called for.

When we started out I noticed the older members of the team falling behind at a slower pace than the young energetic group of us. This was easier than I thought and although I had been cautioned about keeping my pack weight as light as possible, I thought I'd add a little, just to make it challenging.

The first indication I got that it indeed might be a challenge was about two miles into the hike. I definitely began to realize that there was extra weight on my back, and that it was heavy. I then devised the strategy that if I drank some water and ate some of the jelly beans I had brought along for that "instant energy boost," my load would begin to lighten. I knew, in fact, it would have very little effect, but I was working on my "unconscious mental attitude." I had read books about excelling physical barriers by the right positive mental attitude. This strategy worked fine for a while, then the weight of the backpack became real again, not imaginary.

Then I started to notice that the trail was not only winding, but we had to go up and down these hills which were rapidly becoming mountains. Climbing up was labored and hiking down was a constant process of putting on the brakes, much like huge semi-vehicles do on steep grades. For the first time on the hike, "I got in touch with my knees." They were the first to sow the seeds of rebellion, pointing out to me the obvious, about how I should have prepared as the others did. My back quickly followed, complaining about how the extra weight idea wasn't so cute after all. My feet were not exactly overjoyed with my brand new (and expensive) hiking boots which were definitely being "broken in."

It was obvious to me that matters were getting out of hand and we needed to stop, have a conference, and re-group. I don't know why I did this, because every part of my body joined in the rebellion implying that the leadership of this mission (my mind) might be questionable; no, definitely questionable. This was the time for my true leadership qualities to step forward and take charge of this mutinous group with some stirring and patriotic appeal to their sense of duty.

Then my stomach, which was well fed prior to our departure, asked how far had we come? I checked with one of my fellow-hikers, who estimated we had hiked in about three miles. "Three miles!" I exclaimed. "You'd better check again." Then he said, "I was wrong, it's exactly 2.8 miles according to my pedometer." Having to report this finding to the group began to dampen even my idea of the "fun of hiking twelve miles the first time out." It was necessary to simply tell the group the truth, that my mind's conception of the hike and our experience of the hike were not one and the same. Furthermore, perhaps I wasn't the gallant leader I thought I was and maybe my ego was somehow involved.

At this point, my heart stepped forward and suggested that we had a decision to make now that we were more aware of what a twelve-mile hike was going to be like. After all, it had been noncomplainingly pumping fuel faster when climbing up the trail and slowing things down when descending. Given its importance in the physical scheme of things, even my mind agreed (with suspicion) that a group decision and commitment were necessary to accomplish the remainder of the twelve-mile hike. When my heart went back into its unpretentious and nonthreatening mode of operation, something spontaneously happened to my mind. I realized for the first time that we were actually a team and a team effort was required to succeed. Somehow, it didn't seem so important anymore to be the leader and be in control.

When we started out again, all of my body parts appeared to perform out of a sense of we're all in this together; if we all don't make it, then none of us individually do. Needless to say, given this level of joint commitment, we were able to accomplish the hike in such a way that my *concept* of the hike slowly became superimposed with my *experience of the hike*. As this process occurred it also became more enjoyable. I discovered that the more experience and concept were one and the same, the more my concept seemed to disappear. This realization allowed me to become more aware of the wonders of nature around me. Therefore, the hike changed from making it to the campsite to enjoying what was happening to me moment by moment in the process of experiencing.

Aware and Aware/Unaware

What I discovered from my first hiking experience was that, basically, our lives involve two domains of operation of which we are conscious. The first domain involves those aspects of life that we are aware of through experiences. Some of our experiences occur simultaneously with fundamental changes in our perception of the world, i.e., realizations. In any case, this domain is characterized by the fact that we know what we know by actual experience. This experiential domain is represented in Figure 1 by the center circle.

As a result of that hiking experience, I gained valuable realizations about my physical body and its relationship to the control center: my mind. I discovered that there is much to be learned about my true self by listening more often to my body (instead of my mind), without the necessity of a rebellion or some severe illness. I also learned, in a nonintellectual way, that my experiences and my thoughts are separate and distinct. And in some situations, the less thinking I do, the more enjoyable and relaxing life flows.

The second major domain of operation is nonexperiential. It essentially contains beliefs about life for which we generally have no personal experience. We may refer to this domain as that within which we are "aware that we are unaware of by experience." Prior to the hike, I had a concept of what backpacking was like *and* a concept of what my experience of it was going to be. At the point we had the conference was the first time I really began to discover that my thoughts and my experiences were different. The difficulty I had resulted from the fact that my preconceived notions about hiking (which my mind was determined to hold onto) were inconsistent with my reality of hiking (which my body was well aware of). Thus, the solution to this difficulty was first becoming aware of this difference and second creating the opportunity for the realizations I described above to occur.

In a similar manner, if we are aware of some counterproductive behavior we have that seriously interferes with our professional success, and we are unaware of the source, then we can do something about this behavior. Specifically, we may seek some form of professional assistance or the insights of a supportive friend. In the process, we may discover that the source of our counterproductive behavior might have been an unconscious decision that was made as a child.

An example of such an unconscious decision is "You have to work hard in order to make it in life." The origin of this decision may have resulted from a father's unfulfilled expectation of a son's job performance. At the time of the incident, the son may have actually been unconscious (in terms of hearing his father's exact words) during the process of being corrected or berated. He essentially had an "unexperienced experience," in terms of conscious awareness. The process of essentially reliving this experience consciously is sometimes referred to as a recaptured experience. Such a process provides the opportunity for a realization to occur.

If a decision such as the one above leads us to be intolerant of

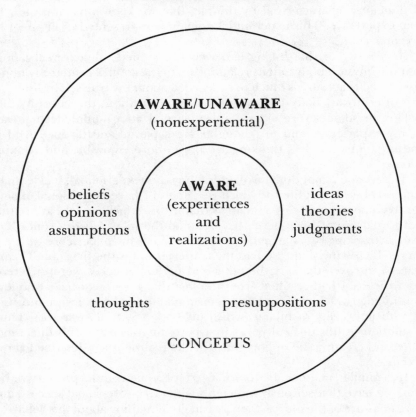

UNAWARE UNAWARE

AWARE/UNAWARE
(nonexperiential)

AWARE
(experiences
and
realizations)

beliefs
opinions
assumptions

ideas
theories
judgments

thoughts   presuppositions

CONCEPTS

Figure 1 The center circle represents what we know by experience and sometimes leads to realizations, i.e., an altered way of being. The second circle represents what we know as a result of having no direct experience. Unaware Unaware represents everything else there is available for us to know.

others who don't work as hard as *we* think this decision requires, then conflict and problems are bound to occur; which in turn interfere with our professional success. Discovering the source and altering our perception of such decisions are almost always accompanied by a recaptured experience, which moves that issue into the center circle of Figure 1. The point here is that we can do something about those aspects of our life which are counterproductive as a result of our concepts, since we are aware that we are unaware of how to solve them ourselves.

After years of attempting to function more effectively and productively by internal changes in organizational structure, with limited success, many businesses and organizations became aware that something more was needed that they were unaware of. In many cases that something involved a new sensitivity by management to the needs of the people who work for businesses and organizations in terms of their significance and well-being.

If I Am Unaware That I Am Unaware, Then I'm Lost

There is a third domain of knowledge that is available to us for which we are unaware that we are unaware of its existence. We refer to this domain as "unaware unaware." This is the domain from which realizations are derived. Quite often, when information acquired from this domain is brought into our personal conceptual domain, it may challenge some presupposition from which we have operated most of our lives. This is the key point at which our open-mindedness is tested. The typical response in the conceptual domain is to have some belief or disbelief about the newly introduced information. As a result, a process is set into motion simply by our willingness to *interact* with this somewhat confronting material *and not by accepting or rejecting it!* Each time an issue is raised that is related to the new information, we view it differently than before we became aware of it. At some subsequent point in time, we may have a permanent shift occur spontaneously in the way we see this issue. It may occur at the time the new information is introduced or some time later after an incubation period. This time span is unique to each individual. That is, it occurs when the individual is either consciously or unconsciously ready. It's like self-paced learning.

In a teacher's workshop, a number of the participants agreed that a severe "problem" was the fact that many students entering college and high school were not adequately prepared. I stated in reply, "I don't understand or see the problem by your statement." They looked at me in a confused manner as if I didn't understand English. I suggested further, "The accurate statement of the situation is that entering students do not meet the *expectations* that we have had for many previous years. The problems we encounter

7

therefore may arise from our expectations in addition to their inadequate preparation." The difficulties that we have had with our attempted solutions to this situation may be in large part due to our viewing this problem solely from the context, "inadequate preparation is the problem."

My attempt to have the group "see" that my statement of the problem revolved around our expectations of incoming students was less than enthusiastically received. Which essentially meant that no solutions derived from this context were available to the group. It's not important in this example whether what I am suggesting is accurate or not, the point is that prior to my statement, such a view of the problem was unaware unaware to most of the group. Those who had a willingness to interact with my assertion had the opportunity for a personal realization and, correspondingly, a radically different solution than those previously attempted. Those who rejected my statement still moved from unaware unaware to the aware unaware circle, where they simply disbelieved what I suggested. Even in this case, the seed planted by my statement meant that realizations could also occur with the latter group, probably at some future time.

Being unaware that we are unaware of some aspect of our life important to our well-being means that there is nothing we can do to help ourselves. Much of the information in this book is derived from this domain based upon my own personal experiences. Let's begin with a more in-depth look at realizations.

Chapter Two

REALIZATIONS

*"When you once see something as false
which you have accepted as true,
as natural, as human,
then you can never go back to it."*

J. Krishnamurti

What Is a Realization?

To *realize* something about yourself is a truly moving experience. To call it an experience and describe it somehow seems to be inadequate – probably because it is inadequate. Such a realization occurred to me in the recent past. It was shortly after I had participated in a workshop in which I was dealing with the area of relationship. As I was driving along the freeway from my home, I was stunned as I had never been before. I had to stop and park on the shoulder of the freeway as the full intensity of what had happened became clear to me. For the first time in my life, I realized that a relationship is fundamentally about an unconditional commitment to someone, something, some idea, etc., and that it did not begin with what do I get from the relationship. My first impulse was to dismiss such a realization as at best, paradoxical, or at worst, nonsense. It was in opposition to everything I had ever learned and experienced about being related. To my initial discomfort, this new way of framing relationship simply would not go away. It was as though I had gone through a door which disappeared the moment I walked through it. Every time I attempted to return to my old way of operating, I felt like a fraud or a liar. I finally came to accept my *altered way of being* in relationships with both personal and professional friends. As a result, the nature of my relationships has taken on a significantly improved quality and, correspondingly, a quantitative reduction in conflict and stress.

Although that occurrence wasn't my first realization, it did leave me shaken and initially quite frightened. It is interesting to note the sequence of events involved in a realization. It appears to be initiated *before* the experience of something happening within the body, such as fear, elation, sadness, etc. Then it is described and ultimately stated in a form somewhat like a definition. Therefore, a realization appears to occur in three distinct stages: initiation, literally outside of time; experience; and the description of what happened.

Quite often, realizations are initiated out of crises which appear to be more threatening to our personal well-being as we are than fundamentally changing our way of being. An example of such a crisis-driven realization happened in one of our workshops to a person whom I'll call Steven. For some years his marriage to Betty had not worked well and it had recently begun to have greater tension and conflict. The situation was brought to a head when Betty insisted on working and Steven was opposed, as he had been for many years. This eventually led to a threatened separation and possible divorce. Faced with this crisis, Steven consented to Betty's working, but he harbored a deep-seated and covert resentment, which threatened to dissolve their marriage.

In a workshop process, *he* discovered that he was often left alone as a child and had always had fears of abandonment. By preventing his wife from working, he unconsciously felt assured of always having her and not being abandoned. As a result of this process, he also discovered that this deeply hidden assumption about abandonment not only involved his wife, but most of his relationships tended to be exclusive and possessive. When his childhood assumption was exposed for examination (by his own discovery), he realized the falsity of it and the source of his counterproductive behavior in relationships. This issue was never the same for him again. Having the realization essentially resolved the true source of the problem. The important point here is that Steven's gradual change in behavior, after the realization, was derived from his altered way of being and not simply by verbal instructions to behave differently.

A fairly common crisis-driven realization happens to many students who attend college out of the insistence of their parents. Some are strongly pushed to be "doctors," "professors," or some other profession the parents believe to be financially sound, respectable, and fulfilling. These are principally supportive parents whose intention is the welfare of their children. Such a student often creates a crisis by performing too poorly academically to merit professional school or simply by performing at a level that results in academic probation. This is the case for many students who have excelled in high school, thus it is not a matter of ability or potential.

This type of crisis naturally raises the question for the student to face, "Do I want to be in college?" The answer is sometimes yes and sometimes no. However, the student is usually forced to claim, for the first time, ownership of her or his decision to be in college. Prior to this realization, the parents are usually held responsible for the student's poor performance and it is justified by statements such as, "I'm only here because my parents insist," "My dad wants me to be a doctor like him," etc. Actually (in spite of their insistence), at a more fundamental level, the parents were never really to blame for their children's poor performance, as we'll discuss in Chapter 4.

One thing is certain about realizations that I have had, they *never* occur until *I* am ready and willing, either consciously or unconsciously. For some years, the issue of my own personal prejudice toward selected groups of people was neatly tucked away and only used on special occasions. As I experienced more people of the world and particularly those I harbored the greatest justified prejudice of, the more difficult it became for me to have so many "special cases" of "You're different from the rest." Simultaneously, I was beginning to extend my way of viewing responsibility to include more and more of the results occurring in my life. That is, I was beginning to live out of a greater sense of ownership and less blaming others.

If I was to make the next quantum jump in my professional career, some new way of viewing myself, with respect to people in general, was required. My old way had simply run its course and within its framework there was only limited but predictable growth and advancement. These considerations generated a state of confusion that lasted for about six months before my breakthrough occurred. Simply stated, "You're not a victim of any system or group of people." Realizations are at first paradoxical and nonsensical. I simply don't question or try to explain them anymore. With this realization came an entirely new world of possibilities which were previously unavailable to me.

Prior to the occurrence of my realization, I had an increasing sense and feeling of fear in my body, although I did not understand the source of it. In retrospect, it is clear to me that giving up my prejudices unconsciously appeared to leave me less able to deal with the world and certainly less protected. The period of confusion involved the process of weighing the security and surety of where I was in comparison to new possibilities that I knew I wanted. The catch is that we can't have the availability of new possibilities until we nonintellectually give up our old restrictive views. It is vital to see that our restrictive views comprise a self-imposed prison, which absolutely prevents any possibilities outside of the beliefs of its framework.

I can always look back on realizations that have occurred with great clarity and see that the timing was of my own doing, even when I was unaware that such was the case at the time. Some type of mysterious communication occurs to spark the process of a new realization, and the result is a more open and accepting way of viewing the world. Thus, the ultimate form of a realization, when subsequently described, is a *concept*. To begin to make a clear distinction between a concept and what happens to us as an experience, is to begin to gain a skill that I believe to be absolutely essential to a quality life, both personally and professionally.

Fear

As I mentioned above, those realizations that have had the greatest impact on me personally have also had varying degrees of fear associated with them. It was as though I also suffered some loss. One of the consequences of the realization I described previously about relationships was that I could no longer credibly operate as I had previously. For example, I could no longer convincingly say to a colleague, "I'm willing to see things your way *only* if you are also willing to see things my way." It was as though I had to have a blind trust in him! In other words, I was losing, to some extent, the surety of what I could expect from him in the future – essentially,

13

giving without expectation. To even consider giving up an expected or known way of operating brings with it fear. But fear of what? Survival! Survival is probably the most fundamental instinct of all human beings. Somehow our fears, both real and imagined, seem to weave their way back to some instinctive statement, "To give up my way of operating (whether productive or not) is associated with loss, and losing threatens my survival."

Another aspect of the fear associated with realizations is the fact that we don't get anything to replace the apparent loss we are due to suffer. It's like giving up something and receiving nothing in return. For example, a logical question would be, "If I'm going to change my way of operating in my personal life because it produces conflict in my relationships, then how should I operate?" If I were to say to you, "I don't have a way for *you* to operate that will ensure a happy and working relationship, but trust *yourself* that giving up your unproductive way of operating will open up an altered way of being that is natural and unique to you," you would probably think I am crazy. When I think about it logically, I would probably also think I am crazy, or at least, suggesting a crazy solution to a real problem.

Much of the unproductive behavior in our relationships results from the apparent necessity to possess and control other individuals. This mode of operation appears to be paramount to our own survival. To allow a relationship freedom is equivalent to freeing ourselves and almost invariably brings with it feelings of fear. The point is that there is fear associated with most realizations. Because they happen spontaneously, we don't get an opportunity to barter for something that is apparently given up or lost.

Sharing Realizations

Probably the most frustrating aspects of having a realization are: first, we are sometimes scared to tell it to other people; and second, when it is safe to do so, it sounds stupid and clumsy in the description. After ten minutes or so of my efforts at explaining a realization to a close friend, his quizzical look tells me he thinks I've suffered some kind of mental aberration from working too hard or taking too many seminars. I begin to consider how I can suavely make it seem like a joke or something that someone else told me. Even to the extent of naming a real person whom we can both agree upon is truly crazy. This frustration is probably one of the clearest indications to me that there is something fundamentally different about my experience (which is clear) and my ability to put my experience into words. To note further, the moment I reduce my experience to a description, it becomes a concept. Concepts typically carry with them interpretation and decision.

Are Realizations Logical?

I guess my inability to accurately describe my experiences or realizations in a logical manner implies that in some instances they probably *are* illogical. However, I am reminded how paradoxical solutions are often used to effect fundamental change in a situation or a person. An example that comes to mind is the workaholic who claims to be seeking a solution to habitual overwork. The analyst, who has an illogical stroke of genius, recommends that the workaholic not only do nothing to curb her overworking behavior, but work harder! Upon taking this advice for a week or so, she becomes incensed at the demand placed on her by the analyst, recovers her own personal responsibility in the matter, and gives *herself* permission "to overwork or not to overwork!"

Therefore, not only are realizations probably impossible to describe accurately, but they are also often illogical, which adds to the difficulty in describing them.

Realizations Are Not Intellectual

The final point about having a realization is that it is not an intellectual exercise. Therefore, it does not require convincing or belief by anyone else. It is a uniquely personal way in which we have an altered sense of ourselves and how we relate to others. It typically results in an expanded understanding of people we relate to in such a way that we truly *see* life from their point of view. Therefore, not only is there nothing intellectual about a realization, but it also does not require our being intellectual in order to have one. Realizations are available to anyone at any moment in time.

15

Chapter Three

IS SURVIVAL THE DRIVING FORCE?

*"Somehow our fears, both real
and imagined, seem to weave their way
back to some instinctive reality.
To change the way I am
(whether productive or not)
is associated with loss, and losing
threatens my survival."*

The Author

Survival Is Innate

I suggested in the previous chapter that realizations have associated with them fear that our survival is somehow threatened. If we view the world from the point of view of an infant, we begin to discover how survival dominates an infant's total activity.

For an infant, the birthing process was probably not only traumatic but certainly created fears of survival, particularly if forceps were used. This process, followed by separation from the mother and gradual adjustment to the external environment, almost certainly causes an infant's actions and reactions to be dominated by survival instincts. Babies learn, eat, play, sleep, communicate, etc., almost totally from the standpoint of survival. They are not interested in recommended feeding schedules when they are hungry. Their crying means, "If I don't get fed, I'll die." Probably other nonverbal statements are, "Please don't stop playing with me," "I'm afraid to be alone," and "I'm wet, what's going to happen to me?" (Since we spend so much time changing their diapers, they probably figure that being wet too long is dangerous.) These are all survival-based reactions.

Over the first twelve months, the central nervous system develops rapidly and things really start to get interesting. Now the baby is ready to learn. However, the only basis for learning at this point is to observe how we adults behave and they probably assume that's what's expected of them. "I have to be like them to be okay, and not get evicted." Babies begin to learn very early what pleases and displeases parents whom they are dependent upon for survival. They simply observe our reactions to their behavior and gradually become aware of what appears to be threatening or non-threatening. Infants dare not do anything which they perceive will seriously jeopardize their survival. And parents are eager and willing to make known to infants and young people what is appropriate and inappropriate about their behavior. This, of course, is probably well known to most of us. Essentially, we want to remind ourselves that survival is innate and that our early behavior, in large part, results from what we consider necessary for survival.

Early Life Decisions

What might not be so well known is that along with our early experiences as infants and young people, we also make *decisions* about our action-response sequence to our environment and those individuals within it. I learned very young that if I looked displeased about something (and didn't push it), people responded in a way to appease my displeasure. "Boy, that worked wonderfully; I think I'll try it again in this other situation." "Wow,

19

that got the same result! This should definitely be stored in my newly acquired box called *survival skills*."

I really want to emphasize here how important and dominant this period is in our lives, for the rest of our lives. Armed with the new skill sequence of experience, interpret, and decide, a young person is ready to take on the world. The basis for the interpretation and decision is again survival, not logic and reason.

An example of how such decisions are made and the subsequent consequences is the following: A young person is running through the house, knocks over a lamp and breaks it. The parent's spontaneous response is, "Be careful, don't be clumsy and stupid." The first thing the child experiences is fear, followed by "you're stupid." Now a decision must be made, either he is stupid and life is about the process of proving this decision, or he decides "I am not stupid," and life is about the never-ending process of proving he is not stupid.

If we take the latter case where "stupid" is the trigger word, much of this person's life may be devoted to performing at an "unstupid" level. However, that is usually not sufficient; he also *requires* acknowledgment that he is not stupid, such as high grades, approval of others, constant stroking, etc. This person may operate out of a never-ending demand for these types of expectations. If these expectations are not met, the non-verbal message they may receive is that they are probably stupid and their relationships are in for difficulties.

The most important point of this example is that much of our present unconscious behavior is based on similar decisions. Incredibly, quite often when people make such discoveries about counterproductive aspects of their behavior, they have absolutely no intention to change.

I decided very early in life that being smart and excelling academically appeared to offer the greatest flexibility and freedom. I was allowed to miss classes, participate in extracurricular activities, received gold stars at the end of each term, and acknowledgments by the truckload. The funny thing I noted about making "A's," which has never been said to me to this day, is that it is also "morally good to make A's." At least that's how I have it put together in my reality. I also notice that we get excused for a lot of weird behavior by being smart. In later life we get the privilege of being called eccentric, which I have interpreted to mean, "See how far you can go before someone gives you the sign that the boundary has been reached!"

As a young person (and even as an adult), I distinctly remember operating out of this decision, which evolved into a personal belief. I later learned how to adorn it with righteous justifications, such as, "I have a perfect right to do what I please (this is America), as long as it doesn't hurt anyone else," or "I have a right to my own privacy," or "What I do in my home (to other people) is a constitutional right," etc. The fact is, almost *everything* I do affects something or someone in some way. By the fact that I am related in some way to those I live and work with, *whatever* I do impacts their lives.

What I want to emphasize here is that we make illogical decisions at very early ages, based on our perceptions that we require those decisions for survival. Many of our decisions are, in fact, necessary for survival. However, many of them are the actual sources of conflicts in our personal and professional relationships.

Practically all of our early life is about the systematic process of experiencing our environment, noting the response, and deciding how that experience affects our survival. If it *appears* to be threatening (and practically all are), we devise some course of action so that if it recurs in the future, we have a plan of action. After a sufficient number of occurrences of a similar-looking experience for which we have devised a refined course of action, our response becomes automatic. It's like learning how to drive. We no longer mentally say for driving a stick shift, "I first depress the clutch, then shift to first, then let up slowly on the clutch, etc."

Essentially, as a five-year-old, out of observation of my parent's interaction, and whom I perceived to win or lose, I decided whom I was going to be like. I decided to be like my mother. My mother would take on the neighborhood, if required, in defense of her children. To me, she was "solid as a rock" and could always be depended upon. There is little question that much of my behavior is predicated on decisions *I* made, derived from experiences with my mother.

There is a vitally important distinction I am making in the previous statement, which involves ownership and responsibility. Notice I said, "*I* decided on the basis of my experiences with my mother," and not simply because I was exposed to her that "I am like my mother." Somewhere in the latter phrase there is a hint of "shared responsibility" simply because my mother was the character who provided the source of my experiences. I am stating that I take full responsibility and ownership for my childhood decisions. Only through total ownership is it possible to effect fundamental change. In fact, I also decided that many aspects of her behavior were not in the best interest of my survival, and these I decided *not* to store in my survival-skills box.

The entire sequence of early life interactions with my mother has, until recently, unconsciously dominated the way I related to women in general. As a five-year-old, I had taken care of relationships with women for the rest of my life! Previously, the thought of being in an intimate relationship with a woman whom I perceived to be like my mother immediately raised fears of losing, which in turn threatened my survival. At present, I am

21

aware that such fears are simply conditioned responses and have no truth in reality.

The fact that we are strongly influenced and conditioned by our parents is well known. The prospect of total ownership of those decisions, both desirable and undesirable, in a nonintellectual way is not so well known or widely accepted.

The Evolution of a Reality

The collection of decisions I made as a young person, based principally on my perceived survival, is the construction of my reality. Essentially, it is the way I view and react to the world. It doesn't really matter to me that many of these decisions may have nothing to do with my survival or that they are sources of unworkability in my relationships. As far as I am concerned, they have literally kept me alive this long and if you expect me to give them up in order to make my relationships work, then I'd rather give up the relationships.

I hope you can now appreciate why my realization about relationships left me so shaken and scared. What I discovered, however, was that any substitution in behavior or way of acting which didn't have any true intent with it wouldn't make any real difference anyway. Therefore, attempting to resolve my problem by simple behavior modification wasn't the answer. Something more was called for. In having this realization, I was literally forced to learn to live with it. In other words, I had to begin to learn how to *do* nothing and learn how to simply *be* natural, since realizations provide no substitute form of behavior. What happened then was a natural way of behaving evolved out of simply being natural in the area of relationships.

If this all sounds confusing, it is to me also; and I refer you to chapter two, describing realizations. It's like swimming for the first time. Before jumping into two feet of water at age five, all the fears, thoughts, and concepts about swimming and dying are real, until you jump in and stand up, and feel like the star in "Tarzan Conquers the Pool."

So what's the point of this chapter? We've all made survival-based decisions as young people that were really survival-imagined. These decisions dominate much of the unworkability in our present everyday life. Fundamental changes through realizations provide a source of recovering our natural way of being. Let's now begin the stepwise process of learning how to discover these decisions and to recover our natural way of being in the most direct manner.

Chapter Four

RESPONSIBILITY IS SYNONYMOUS WITH OWNERSHIP

"When we treat man as he is, we make him worse than he is. When we treat him as if he already were what he potentially could be, we make him what he should be."

Goethe

What Is Responsibility?

As you might have guessed by now, giving up old acquired habits, which to some extent might have served us in the past, is not a simple task. It requires intent and willingness on our part. As a basis, it requires us to be *responsible*. Responsibility, as used here, is the willingness to see ourselves as the source of the conditions and circumstances in our lives. Responsibility actually goes beyond simply admitting and accepting the conditions associated with our lives; it also means owning and possessing the results we have been producing, both personally and professionally. It is only out of this sense of ownership that it is possible to have responsibility become real and not conceptual.

When this level of responsibility is applied to some situation in our life that we resist owning totally, a deeply personal process begins to occur. An example which readily comes to mind is the first time someone suggested to me that as a teacher I was 100 percent responsible for the results produced in my class. I immediately responded by asking, "What about the students' responsibility? Don't they share that 100 percent with me?" The reply was, "They have a separate 100 percent responsibility that is independent of yours. Students are 100 percent responsible for their learning." Needless to say, this way of viewing responsibility was, at best, new to me, and, at worst, a foreign concept. I had always viewed responsibility as being shared.

There is another way of making the same point, and one I often use in my "Responsibility Workshops." In order to be able to influence or control something, we must first be willing to own it. If it's out of our hands or outside of us, there's little we can do except hope and pray. It's like sitting in the back seat of a moving car hoping that it doesn't run off the road and shouting, "Somebody do something!" Then there's a voice on the intercom saying, "Why don't *you* do something? All you have to do is climb into the front seat and take control of the steering wheel with the big 'R' on it."

Taking charge of our lives is essentially the process of assuming 100 percent responsibility for the results we produce. I am aware that this is not an easy pill to swallow. I stated above that students are totally responsible for their learning. Viewed from this perspective, it makes little difference if an instructor is sympathetic, apathetic, understanding, dictatorial, uninformed, etc. The student realizes and accepts responsibility for seeking the information and experiences relevant to being educated. I view education as *empowering students to think and do for themselves*, or the process of producing fully functional individuals. Anything less is demeaning to a student.

In terms of accountability, instructors are responsible for approaching students from the standpoint of being whole, complete, capable, and perfect just as they are. How a student is framed is typically how they will turn out, at least in the instructor's reality. Recall our discussion of "inadequately prepared students" in Chapter 1.

I know you are probably saying, "But there are situations in my life where the outcome does depend on others or a team effort in order to create a workable situation." I acknowledge that such situations are, in fact, true. I would suggest, however, that what is required of us (as I indicated at the start of this chapter) is to *look for* how much more we are willing to own rather than looking for examples which are used to prove that viewing responsibility in this way is not universal.

Ego As a Barrier to Responsibility

When I examined carefully my experience of teaching, I realized that much of it involved assumptions and concentration on myself. As an example, I assumed when I walked into a classroom with a captive audience of students that learning was going to occur, simply because I had such valuable material to present that was vital to the students' survival. I subsequently discovered that they learned whether I showed up or not, or whether they showed up or not! Much of my preoccupation during presentations was with, "How well am I doing this derivation?" "I hope no one asks a question I can't answer," "I wonder if they think I am as smart as I pretend to be," etc. These were basically unconscious questions that dominated the context of a lecture. Not only were they obviously ego-driven, but they were used to protect me from being exposed as someone actually pretending to be bright.

Another common technique used for this purpose is the proverbial "snow-job," i.e., the presentation of material one or two levels above the students' grasp. I began to *see* that keeping students off balance (unconsciously) was really a defense mechanism. These discoveries were very sobering to me and critically challenged my willingness to be responsible at the apparent expense of my ego. In fact, for the first time, I began to understand a comment made to me some years ago by a friend, which was, "Teaching is 99 percent ego and 1 percent exhibitionism." My guess is that most of my colleagues would probably think this statement is 99 percent ridiculous and 1 percent intellectually discussable. Maybe we ought to ask students one of these days.

As I began to assume greater responsibility for the results being produced in my classes, the students magically began to respond and appear interested. I must admit I really don't know exactly how it works; but the more I assumed the responsible role, the better things seemed to work. Essentially, what I did was to begin viewing the world through the eyes of those I worked with. At regular intervals throughout my written lecture, there were questions such as, "What's going on with them?" or "Are they interested or bored?" just to remind myself to note where my attention was and that it's a privilege to be responsible for the teaching and well-being of others.

You're probably saying by now, "Okay, I'm willing to consider being responsible, but where do I begin? Do I bend over backwards and let people walk all over me?" To discover ways of being more responsible is easy; to *not do something* about it is the tough part. The reason is that *being more responsible involves giving up some behavior, belief, attitude, etc., rather than concentrating on behaving a different way.* Again, we are faced with giving up as a loss, and the loss threatening our survival. In order to illustrate this point, we begin this process by considering ways we commonly and unconsciously use for avoiding responsibility.

One of the most common techniques we use for avoiding responsibility is to become upset. Obviously, if we're upset, we can't handle the matter. Have you ever noticed how conveniently we become upset at times crucial to the consideration of substantive issues? Becoming upset is a *classic* in the arsenal of defense mechanisms. We all use it. There is always a choice of whether to be upset or to take responsibility. The next time you find yourself upset at someone or something, stop and privately ask yourself the question, "How, why, or for what am I avoiding being responsible?"

Going unconscious, sometimes known as "Going south when I should be going north," is an ideal mechanism we use for avoiding responsibility. This is classically done by simply tuning someone out. It is also done by having your own mental conversation while someone is attempting to point out how you could have assumed greater responsibility.

Playing the role of victim is another mechanism we use to escape being responsible. A common characteristic of the victim role is disablement. Being a victim implies an individual is less than fully functional. Expressions common to a victim are "I can't," "I'm unable," etc. These statements are really, "I am unwilling."

Just in the process of living, we need only become more aware of our everyday behavioral patterns as illustrated by the three previous examples in order to assume greater responsibility. The quality of our life is directly proportional to the extent to which we take responsibility for the conditions and circumstances that are present.

Levels of Responsibility

In summary, we consider the levels of responsibility and where we each find ourselves operating:

27

Level 1

We essentially see ourselves at the mercy of our environment. We consistently experience unwanted results in our life and are unwilling to face the truth about the cause. This level is also characterized by an unyielding and fixed attitude about life, having no space for openness and consideration. Our view of life is essentially absolute; an Archie Bunker type comes to mind.

When operating from this level, much of life is experienced out of the role of being a victim, with characteristic statements such as, "How could this happen to me?" "Why me?" "If I could just get lucky," etc. This person's life is dominated by explanations, reasons, and justifications about why life is not turning out to be like she or he expected.

The result is a feeling of being consistently frustrated with consistently predictable unwanted results.

Level 2

We begin to observe that at least we are always around when we get these unwanted results. Thus, we begin to suspect that we might have something to do with the results in our lives. This level is also characterized by our recognition that similar-looking situations have occurred previously. Therefore, we begin to suspect that some fundamental change in our behavior could have some influence in avoiding the same result in the future.

Typically, some traumatic incident or crises may occur and we decide on some more responsible course of action in order to avoid Level 1 results in the future. It's like the Paul Simon song; once you decide, "There must be fifty ways to leave your lover." The new course of action usually involves risk and trial and error initially, the results of which are sometimes the source of confusion. The significance of this confusion is the fact that the unyielding way we previously viewed an issue is undergoing change and movement, accompanied by a mixture of wanted and unwanted results. There is also a willingness to confront fears, in spite of the fact that there may be blame, fault, and guilt. This is the level at which we consider counseling or some form of workshop or seminar, possibly a self-help book, or simply sharing with someone we trust.

The results we begin to derive from "being in control" of our lives are both exhilarating and scary. The new person that comes into being soon loses memory of the old struggling self. Friends begin to comment that, "You're different," and perhaps scary to them. They become genuinely concerned about your well-being and wonder if you are truly okay, or just on a temporary high. As Helen Keller said, "Life begins to look like a daring adventure. . ."

28

Level 3

We take responsibility for the conditions and circumstances in our life. Occasionally we go back into Level 2, but by and large we experience desirable results in our life.

This level is characteristic of people who see themselves at the fulcrum of life, being the source of that which occurs in their life. It is indicative of those individuals we describe as being successful. Not in terms of the agreed upon "symbols of success," such as money, recognition, acknowledgment, status, etc., but in terms of consistently and purposefully achieving the goals they establish for themselves. The only way this type of quality is available is through ownership of and responsibility for that quality.

Level 4

Service is the level of human activity where we take responsibility for any human condition which does not contribute to the growth, productivity, and well-being of those involved and we transform that condition into a context which produces workable solutions. Although notable examples are Mother Teresa, Martin Luther King, Helen Keller, Albert Schweitzer, and Mahatma Gandhi, this level is also typical of people we experience daily, such as the neighborhood service-station owner, educator, health professional, secretary, computer analyst, housewife, etc. This level is basically about contribution to others with no expected payoff.

Based on the discussion of the last two sections, we can begin to see that life is constantly providing opportunities for us to consider and confront those aspects of our behavior which are counterproductive. All that is required is a willingness on our part to engage the process at whatever pace is individually appropriate. As an aid in this process, the next chapter helps us make a clear distinction between our long-held behavior patterns and our individual self-worth as human beings.

Chapter Five

DISTINGUISHING EXPERIENCE FROM INTERPRETATION

"Since everything in life is but an experience perfect in being what it is, having nothing to do with good or bad, acceptance or rejection, one may well burst out in laughter."

Long Chen Pa

Introduction

This is one of the most important discussions in the book. It deals with how to consistently and purposefully produce desired results, both personally and professionally. In order to derive the maximum benefit from the material that will be discussed, we're going to have to really concentrate. We begin this discussion by examining the extent to which we are aware of our ability to distinguish our experiences from our interpretations of them. Then I will introduce an entirely different level of existing that will make a corresponding difference in our living. The realization of this level is challenging in that it involves a willingness to *let go* of present thoughts, ideas, judgments, evaluations, etc., a literal cessation of present mental activity. J. Krishnamurti[1] describes it as "quieting the mind." This is a realm of which most of us have somehow been aware, but unaware of how to avail ourselves of it on a consistent basis. The process of distinguishing these realms is the essential requirement for understanding this discussion and gaining value. I would, however, like to point out that *understanding* this discussion is an intellectual exercise and is altogether different from utilizing it. This difference is discussed in detail in the course of this chapter.

It's a Matter of Distinction

To make distinctions about life is probably fundamental to human beings. It is certainly used in the process of acquiring and classifying knowledge. To make a distinction is the act of differentiating between or among things; it is also the act of recognizing and becoming aware of differences that are not consciously known. Each of us could transform the quality of our life by the simple willingness to make a distinction between our concepts of life and our experiences of life. Let's pause for a moment and give some thought to the previous statement. Our ability to recognize distinctions between people we live and work with is vital to the way we interact with them individually and, correspondingly, to the results we are able to produce in relationships with each of them.

For the most part, this type of distinguishing is rather straightforward. However, what is not so straightforward, or ordinarily conscious to most of us, are our unconscious opinions of people we live and work with, and the extent to which these opinions drive our experiences of them. It's like having *programmed experiences*. The experience is consistent with the program.

As an exercise, you might make a list of specific individuals you live or work with. Then, for each of them, write a list of ten (10) words that spontaneously come to mind. Don't censor any words; this is a private exercise! These words are the basis of your concept of those individuals.

33

When developed into refined form, it is your unconscious reality of them, and *it* drives your experience of them.

Based on the previous discussions, this isn't too difficult to see. Our early life is essentially about building a system of beliefs based on experiences. We then systematically collect evidence to reinforce our self-consistent body of beliefs, and they become a closed system called " our reality." Literally, everything in our consciousness is a "construct of theories" about real events. This is usually the point at which most people start to get a headache. It shouldn't surprise you to know that just writing about this subject gives me a headache! Hang in there with me. I stated at the start that this discussion wasn't going to be easy.

The problem here is twofold: First, we construct our realities at a time when we have no idea or appreciation of logic or common sense. Second, the system we construct is based, for the most part, on what appears to be survival.

Have We Been Making This Distinction?

Let's take a closer look at the distinction I am making by the use of examples in each category shown in Table 1.

Our total accumulated knowledge may be characterized, according to Karl Popper,[2] by knowledge of physical objects and phenomena, states of consciousness or mental states, such as beliefs and opinion, etc. (subjective knowledge); and objective contents, such as laws of the universe, theories, etc. (objective knowledge). This knowledge is stored in our brains, and recalled as concepts. Processing in the experiential realm refers to the act of actually carrying out some method, technique, or process. The act of doing something.

For example, the processes of walking, swimming, driving, etc., are all experiential while they are happening. When they are completed, we refer to them in conceptual form as I took a walk, a swim, a drive, etc. While they are occurring moment by moment, we refer to these as acts of processing; that is, simply carrying out a process.

For every experience I have, there is a conscious or unconscious interpretation of it, which becomes a concept subsequent to the experience. For example, before I had the experience of skiing, it was a mental picture to me based on my exposure to reading, television, hearsay, etc. When I actually put on a pair of skis and learned through experience, my picture was significantly altered. It is also important to note that my mental picture could equally well have been validated.

The point to be made here is that every experience we have, in the moment-by-moment process of living, is ultimately *represented* by a descrip-

EXPERIENCE
Processing
Feelings
Emotions
Intuition
Use of the
Five Senses

CONCEPTS
of our
TOTAL ACCUMLATED KNOWLEDGE

Physical Objects and Phenomena

People	Earthquakes
Furniture	Experiments
Mountains	Sunrise
Rivers	Rain
Sun	Snow

Subjective Knowledge

Beliefs	Attitudes
Opinions	Ideas
Judgments	Thoughts
Views	Evaluations

Objective Knowledge

Music	Theories
Laws	Proofs
Poetry	Skills
Mathematics	Solutions
Techniques	Information

Table 1 The realm of knowledge recalled or unexperienced is conceptual and is clearly distinguished from the realm of moment-by-moment experiencing.

tion. Thus, we can begin to see that this is a representational realm. The concept of skiing is certainly distinct from the experience of skiing. The memory of skiing is stored in my brain, and recalled through thinking in conceptual form. In a like manner, the experience of feelings and emotions is certainly distinct from the manner in which we ultimately describe them.

At certain times and on certain occasions we experience sensations about certain people in our lives which are undescribable and unexplainable. The inadequate statement we typically use for communicating these feelings and emotions is "I love you." I don't know about you, but this simple statement, in spite of its power, has appeared to be inadequate to me in certain situations. It's as though no number or combination of words could truly communicate my feelings in terms of a conceptual verbal statement. There was always something missing. That something which was missing is the distinction between experience and concept; and that which is missing suggests a discontinuity between the two operational realms.

However, most of us not only make no distinction between the experiential and conceptual realms, but we operate in life, to a large extent, as if they were superimposed or one and the same. This is essentially a process of living life out of our preconceptions; and, therefore, life is about collecting proof through experiences to validate our preconceptions. Thus we have conceptually derived experiences. Very rarely do we experience people without presuppositions and judgments. This manner of living is indicative of Level 1 responsibility referred to in Chapter 3.

Life is experienced almost totally out of the absolute certainty of a construct of concepts. We can have significantly new insights just by our willingness to begin seeing that because we believe it to be so doesn't make it so. Since many of our beliefs are based on agreement with others, we must remember that during Columbus' time there was almost total agreement that the planet was flat, but that didn't make it so; neither did it stop Columbus from embarking on his voyage.

If the experiential and the conceptual realms were the only two available to human beings, then we should have no problem in having our life work to our individual satisfaction. All we would have to do is discover the ultimate solution predicated upon our total accumulated knowledge or the ultimate process based upon experience, and life should turn out as we wish on a consistent basis. However, this is certainly contrary to experience.

Using a given approach, sometimes things work and sometimes they don't. Presently in education, we are back to basics *again* – and education is going to work! Is it really? With the recent emphasis on basics, we will definitely observe an increase in content acquisition, such as higher SAT and ACT scores, etc., but the "rediscovered" emphasis will hardly empower students to think and do for themselves; the latter is my view of education.

Therefore, something beyond our past and present concepts is called for in order to consistently produce desired results.

When I have had realizations, the source was certainly not my concepts. If the experience were the driving force, I should be wise beyond my years, and I am not. I am obviously suggesting that another level of existence is called for beyond experience and concept. Actually, many writers and philosophers down through history have made reference to a realm beyond experience and concept.

Being Natural and Being Normal

I refer to this realm as a *natural way of being* as contrasted with our *normal way of being*. The simple diagram in Figure 2 describes the alternative ways we experience life.

The terms *normal* and *natural* are used here to basically distinguish behavior which is conceptually derived from that which is not, respectively. Furthermore, I am suggesting that most of our behavior with each other is normal, resulting from survival-based concepts.

Within the framework of this diagram, a realization results in an altered way of being from normal to natural about a given situation. Having a realization does not guarantee, in and of itself, that our behavior will change for the better, although in most cases it does. It means, specifically, that we now have a new insight we did not previously have, which allows an expanded quality of living. We still, however, have a choice of behavior. But, no matter what behavioral pattern we choose, the way we viewed the same or similar situations in the past will be permanently altered and in accord with the realization.

Being is about the way we "view" our experience prior to the experience, and is meaningful only to the extent that it is coupled to some subsequent experience. Therefore, in spite of the fact that being and experiencing are distinctly different realms, they are inextricably coupled. Being normal is basically experiencing life from survival and is often and regularly necessary. Being natural allows new experiences. Being normal is principally driven out of concepts and decisions from the past. Being natural occurs spontaneously when we let go of our thoughts of "how it should be," "how it could be," "how it ought to be," etc., and just allow it "to be like it is."

An example of being natural is visiting Europe for the first time and allowing each event to unfold in an unexpected or spontaneous manner. We are natural to the extent we can let go of our evaluations, judgments, opinions, etc., about each event. When visiting Paris, a statement resulting from a normal way of being may be "Parisians are unfriendly exactly as I was told." From an experience of being natural, a statement may be, "I

37

| Natural way of being | ⇨ | Experience | | ◁ | Normal way of being |

⇩

Accumulated total knowledge (Concepts)

Being natural allows new experiences which becomes knowledge in the form of concepts.	Being normal is basically experiencing life from survival and is sometimes necessary.
Being natural is a requirement for creativity.	Being normal is principally driven out of concepts and decisions from the past.
Being natural occurs spontaneously when one lets go of concepts of the way it should be, could be, ought to be, etc.	Being normal is basically acting as a result of the thought process.

Figure 2   The Being Natural – Being Normal Model

A realization is a discovery about a normal way of being that results in a natural way of being. "Being" is the way we "view" our experience prior to the experience.

was overwhelmed by the sight of the Notre Dame at night." Since it is practically impossible to consistently be natural for any sustained period of time, we are sometimes natural and sometimes normal.

An example that illustrates a personal realization which altered my way of being from normal to natural is the way I used to handle reports written by my staff. I would always ask them to write the "first draft" and I would use that as a basis for the "final draft." The implication was that they were incapable of writing a final draft and that somehow I was indispensable to the process. This is a common characteristic of those of us who refuse to delegate responsibility with decision-making power. The reports had to come back in a form identical to how I would have written them, which is the "hook," since no one else could operate out of my head. No matter how eloquent the explanations given to justify this position, I am clear that this was a normal way of being with my staff and that I was operating out of a view in which they were less than capable and only partially functional. No matter what the unique reasoning framework we have for this mode of operation, it ultimately goes back to our ego.

When this characteristic of mine was first pointed out to me in a workshop, there was the usual denial and the "how could you say that about me" response. When the facilitator wouldn't buy that, I went into my academic routine, sounding very authoritative and professional. She didn't buy that one either. Then I appealed to her caring instincts as a woman. No dice. Then I became very angry because I was running out of routines. The world was literally closing in on me. Then a stroke of genius hit me – pretend what she's saying is true and you are willing to be open-minded. Guess what: she was waiting for me at the pass. There I sat, dumb and dumbfounded. Then she said, "This is an opportunity, Bill."

I don't know exactly what functionally happened, but something switched inside of me and I realized for the first time that my issue was about "doing it my way." This was the first time I had been assisted in actually *seeing* this characteristic of mine and been allowed the opportunity to acknowledge the truth about the matter.

Afterwards, I felt a great sense of relief and a feeling that I had unloaded a very heavy burden. The very next week I called my staff in and apprised them of the new procedure; namely, I was no longer going to rewrite the reports and baby them. From then on, I wanted final reports submitted to me, because I had more important things to do.

What's important to note in this example is the stepwise process of going through each of my explanations before really getting to the issue, which was *control*. The instant before the switch occurred, I could see clearly that my explanations had no real foundation in truth. The key point here is that we have to ultimately come to the point of acknowledging the truth about an issue. Not intellectually, but really seeing the truth about the way we operate as a prerequisite to fundamental change in our behavior. This is an overpowering experience and the self that emerges is truly empowered.

This example reminds me of something I read somewhere – that *in order to be truly free to live, the old self must die.* I also had a choice, after realizing that my staff was perfectly capable and that I was into my ego, whether to continue as before and know consciously it was a lie or to give up my previous way of operating and simply let that part of myself die.

Being Natural Comes Without Effort

Fundamentally, being natural is not about doing something and certainly not about thoughts. It's about where we come from, about our intent, and about who we are and the expression of ourselves to the world. Carl Rogers[3] has written an entire book about this level of existence, titled "A Way of Being." Abraham Maslow[4] has also written a series of descriptions that are indicative of a person who experiences life naturally rather than normally. The following are some examples: more integrated, less split; more open to experience, less fearful; more spontaneous and expressive; ego transcended; closer to the core of being; more natural; trust their own intuition, emotions, and thoughts; more self-accepting; and a "fully functional person."

A practical way of becoming more aware of when we are being natural or normal is by the constant process of observing the results we produce, personally and professionally. And then honestly asking ourselves, "What was my intent?" In the example above I discovered my true intent, underneath it all, was to retain control. This realization allowed me to make a very significant discovery. That is, *we have ultimate control out of a complete absence of control.*

If you try using this approach in examining your behavior, don't settle for the first explanations you come up with. Your mind is much too smart to be fooled that easily. Keep pushing yourself and extend the process over several days if necessary. When you start to get outrageous suggestions (from yourself), such as, "I really did sabotage the evening with my mate when she or he didn't agree with my suggested activity," "I truthfully don't perform well at my job because I simply don't want to be there," "When I look beneath all of my considerations, I have no intention of this relationship working unless certain conditions are met first," etc., begin to consider them very closely. If you are really courageous and serious about discovery, have a truly insightful friend make suggestions to you about what he or she thinks your true motives are.

Another technique I have used for increasing my awareness of where

40

I am coming from is *to compare my declarations with my performance*. Simply stated: "Is what I say what I do?" Is my way of being making promises either that I can't keep or have no intention of keeping? The in-depth examination of broken promises is an excellent opportunity to discover major obstacles to our natural way of being.

An illustration of this point is a person who constantly volunteers to help other people. Quite often this person "overbooks" his or her activities and is either unable to fulfill an agreement or simply does not show up for an appointed date. Afterwards, there is typically an elaborate sequence of events which very justifiably prevented this person from keeping his or her promise. One of the major sources of this behavioral pattern, initiated by making promises, is the need of this person to be either approved of or loved. The awareness of the relationship between approval and broken promises in driving this undesirable behavioral pattern provides the opportunity for this person to overcome such an obstacle and recover his or her natural way of being.

What's important to recognize here is that we are all relatively new at being natural and this talent must be gradually developed and mastered. In the next chapter, we will expand on the concepts introduced in Figure 2 in order that we have a fully understood basis for the practical discussions of relationships, problems and stress, communication, and creativity in the chapters following.

Chapter Six

KNOWLEDGE AND REALITY

"I act and react to the world on the basis of what I know, whether what I know is real or not."

The Author

The useful aspect of the natural/normal diagram illustrated in the previous chapter is that we know where we are coming from at any moment: either a natural or a normal way of being. What I would like to do in this chapter is to develop, in more detail, the nature and implications of that model.

How Do I Know What I Know?

Let's focus for the moment upon the totality of our accumulated knowledge, which Krishnamurti[1] refers to as the *content of consciousness*. Knowledge stored in our brain in the form of concepts, information, and skills is derived from personal experiences, accepted and accumulated knowledge, inherited knowledge, etc., and what is referred to as the *ego*. As individuals, we view life principally through the filter of this conditioning, as diagrammed in Figure 3.

As we can see, practically all of our inherited knowledge is probably truly necessary for survival. This is knowledge in the realm of evolutionary adaptation and preventing extinction of the human species. I am sure most of us would agree that the requisite knowledge and technology exist to ensure that extinction is not a problem.

The category of accepted and accumulated knowledge is probably a combination based on true and imagined survival. For example, training ourselves in some capacity, be it formal education or otherwise, is the least complicated way of ensuring that our inherited necessities are satisfied. On the other hand, having a belief that some people are inherently superior to others is probably based totally on a decision of imagined survival. By the way, the *use* of this concept has no racial distinction. We all use it to gain advantage or profit. Quite often there is confusion between our inherent self-worth as human beings, which we are all awarded by being born, and the unique talents of individuals to perform in an exemplary manner at given tasks.

Perhaps we should use this opportunity to make a very important point. That is, superior/inferior is an example of what I call an *issue* for the person believing or not believing either one of these positions. They are the opposite sides of the same coin. One brings the other into existence. Having one position or the other really makes no difference. This is somewhat paradoxical at first thought, but makes sense the more you think about it.

Individuals with this issue can never achieve enough to be truly superior. Life for them is the never-ending process of proving superiority. If they stop to rest for any length of time, they would be discovered and exposed! The only way out of an issue that runs us is to make it okay to

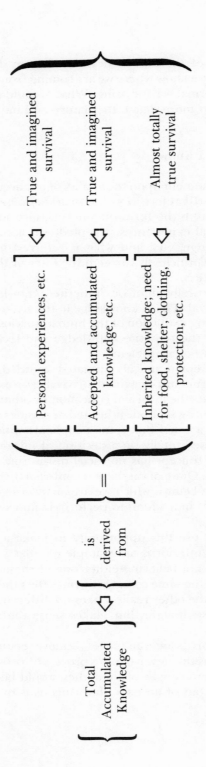

Figure 3 Our total accumulated knowledge is derived from a combination of true and imagined survival sources.

be that which we resist – in this case, inferior. Paradoxical again. We have to be willing for it to be okay to be inferior, before *we* can allow ourselves not to be inferior. Note I didn't say we have to *be* inferior, but *to have it be okay* to be inferior, in whatever manner we have uniquely conceptualized the issue of inferiority.

Trying not to be inferior by being superior is a losing battle. We will always be at the effect of it. Those of us who have been in the trenches for some years will recognize what I'm talking about. We know the relief that comes from letting go of the physical and psychological demands necessary to maintain that front. I sometimes refer to this issue as the *achiever's cycle*, because we always return to "go" in pursuit of a new goal, driven out of the necessity to prove we are not, in fact, inferior by performing and achieving superior feats.

There is an alternative way of achieving and excelling which is not driven out of the necessity to be superior. It could be described by the expression "friendly competition," where we don't confuse the pursuit as being dependent on survival. It's like being on a parallel track and not constantly observing a competitor with suspicion, envy, and distrust. There is an atmosphere of sharing and mutual support. In a like manner, this way of being in competition brings with it a sense of satisfaction and contribution, rather than the disabling consequences of stress.

The category of personal experiences and the decisions resulting from them have been discussed in part in Chapter 2. This category is the world of mental states with behavioral dispositions to act. Knowledge in this sense is, in large part, subjective. If our personal experiences have been mostly about unconsciously acting out childhood decisions, then simply growing older does not necessarily lead to maturity. If, for example, we decide that *fire can be dangerous to our survival*, based upon a personal childhood incident which involved playing with matches, then such a decision is probably true.

If, on the other hand, we decided that *telling the truth in relationships leads to rejection*, based upon incidents where, as young people, we were discouraged from sharing our true feelings, emotions, and confusions, then such a decision is imaginary with respect to survival.

As another example, I decided at a very young age that it was of vital importance to me to be first at everything. There was essentially nothing that I attempted for which the requirement was less than "numero uno." This drive has been referred to as the "drum-major instinct." It was clearly obvious to me that you didn't get to be acknowledged or invited to be on the "Today Show," "Tonight Show," or the "Day After Tomorrow Show" by being "numero duo."

Decisions such as these play a dominant role in determining our behavior in relationships, communication, and in the most important areas of self-esteem and full self-expression. Recovery of these unconscious decisions and reexamination of them is really the subject to which this book is addressed.

Fundamental Life Principle

Of all the illogical decisions we make as young people, there is usually one which is dominant. This decision is essentially the driving force of our individual lives and is called a *fundamental life principle*. Most of us operate in life out of a fundamental life principle. This principle is adopted early in life, typically out of some traumatic incident which appears to threaten our survival. It is adopted with no logic, consciousness, or relationship to true reality, but simply out of some decision that involves our real or imagined survival.

Examples of fundamental life principles are: "Be Intelligent," "Be Strong," "Be Appropriate," "Be Well Thought Of," "Be Nice," "Work Hard," "Get Approval," "Be Macho," etc. What's important to understand is that we *come to* life from our fundamental life principle. We don't challenge or judge our fundamental life principle. It literally runs us. Everything we do, say, feel, or express is dictated by it. In fact, our basic life principle is the expression of who we *think* we really are. It is obvious, when operating from our adopted life principle, that we are totally at the effect of it.

For a person whose life principle is dominated by "approval," he (she) would *never* consider attending a function without the proper attire. He (she) would avoid at all costs any possible scandal or embarrassing situation by any family member, even at the expense of the family member being banished on the pretext that it's in their best interest! This person is very sensitive to statements which are, in general, not complimentary; has an extremely high threshold in terms of self-esteem and full expression; tends to be introverted, no matter how extroverted they may appear; when you think about it, you know very little about this person. He (she) is not a risk taker and is seeking desperately to let go of most of these barriers, but the fear of being exposed and disapproved of is too overwhelming. The necessity for approval is probably one of the dominant characteristics of people in most societies.

The person whose life principle is centered about "being intelligent" is involved in a never-ending process of demonstrating his or her brilliance. It's not too difficult to understand why he or she would probably resist giving up the necessity to *always* appear intellectual; after all, she (he) has a lifetime invested in this way of acting. This person's life principle has essentially become an expression of who she (he) really thinks she (he) is. The principle and the person become one and the same.

We can clearly begin to see how the array of choices, attitudes, characteristics of personality, etc., are all consistent with our fundamental life principles. At this point we first begin to get the hint that we may not have been running things all along, even when we thought we had. To realize that we may not have been controlling our destinies all along is the first step to really being in control. Since we have a clearer picture of how we got here, we can now truly be the author of where we go from here. Even more exciting, to discover your fundamental life principle is to open up the possibility of personally discovering who you really are!

If you trace your life very carefully, you can begin to get some idea of what makes you run. As a result of personally working through this process, I have discovered that my fundamental life principle is centered around the issue of *freedom*. This issue has dominated my life in every aspect – from choice of profession to my "modus operandi" in relationships.

The incident that precipitated this decision in my life is as clear to me as if it had happened yesterday. I was about five years old. I was getting on the bus with my mother and ran to the first available seat while she paid the fares. Since the bus was segregated, this was not where we were supposed to sit and she very sternly made me know that we were moving to a different place. I was shocked and embarrassed, and also felt humiliated. Everyone on the bus saw me chastised for nothing involving wrongdoing. I am totally clear *now* that that was not her intent. In fact, I can remember the anguished look on her face, I imagine for being placed in such a dilemma. Nevertheless, seeing that incident through my eyes as a five-year-old was the ultimate threat, up to that time, to my freedom of choice. Right then and there I decided, no matter how hard I had to work, I would not let my freedom be denied again!

After that incident, there were more similar-looking ones that confirmed my "astute observation" that *they* were out to deny me my freedom. Freedom, since that time, has been the overriding issue in my life. I like the way John Powell[5] expresses it: "The life principle runs through the fabric of our choices like the dominant theme in a piece of music, it keeps recurring and is heard in different settings."

Consistent with this dominant theme, I earned excellent grades in grammar and high schools and, although my family had no money saved for it, there was no question – I was going to college (I earned a scholarship). Education was the route to true freedom. I went to graduate school, earned a Ph.D. and threw in a postdoctoral fellowship.

I was bound to be free soon. I could go back home, get on that bus, sit anywhere I wanted to, and sing, "Free at last, free at last, thank God Almighty, I'm free at last!" Not just yet, though, because I had to teach at a university (where true freedom exists). I had to move through the ranks:

49

Assistant, Associate, and finally, Full Professor. Then I had to do something truly *transformational* in physical chemistry to achieve and deserve ultimate freedom. I was simply acting out one of many possible scripts, all having the same unattainable end, "freedom through achievements."

I think you get the idea now how this one area of my life, involving professional choices, was something I decided for myself at age five. I was simply acting out a script. You might also take a look at events in your life and discover characteristics that may relate to your personal fundamental life principle.

Construction of a Reality

I'm afraid the news doesn't get better just yet. For each area or aspect of life, we evolve from our fundamental life principle an array of decisions, attitudes, and judgments about situations in life, sometimes referred to as a "wiring system."

For example, when I mention to people around the country that I live in Utah and am non-Mormon, most questions and comments are usually about the difficulties I experience. When I say that Salt Lake is one of the best cities I have lived in and *my* experience with the people is one of genuineness and honesty, there is almost always surprise and sometimes disappointment. Even though most of these people have never been to Utah, they do have a reality about it, based on no personal experience.

The point here is that we *come from* our predisposed concepts, depending on how we have it wired. It is vitally important to note that the totality of our concepts relating to every aspect of life is also consistent with our fundamental life principle. They are like the ribs (concepts) connected to the spine (fundamental life principle).

The system of wiring we all have defines our individual realities. Thus, by definition, my reality is different from yours; what we have, in part, are mutually incompatible realities, simply because the array of decisions I have made are not identical to yours, even about similar incidents. This is also a rational explanation for the widely different personalities of children who are raised in the same family and are exposed to essentially identical situations.

In this system of survival-based realities, conflict is inevitable. Thus, instead of working agreements, we often have conflicts and compromises. I define compromise as giving in to that which we don't really agree with, and agreeing, as giving up a position or point of view with no memory of loss or "you owe me next time." An interesting aspect about compromising, however, is that for every inch of compromise, there is produced a corresponding inch of resentment; no matter how unconscious or suppressed. Resentment always brings with it, "I'll catch back," "You owe me," etc.

50

Maybe not on a conscious level, but it's there; and when we do ultimately catch back, we don't have to be responsible for the outcome – it was our turn.

An example that comes to mind is the process my girlfriend and I go through sometimes on deciding on a movie. If I introduce the idea of a certain movie and she feels strongly about another one, we sometimes compromise on one we both think we won't dislike too much. I know I resent having to see the compromise movie, and I catch back by deciding not to like it and being distant with her. Sometimes I justify my position with mental statements like, "It was my idea; why did she have to change the movie?" "The movie I wanted to see had a really important *message* we could have both benefited from," etc.

Basically, my unique mode of catchback is to withhold my support and love until I think she's suffered enough! The really frustrating part of this entire situation is that my girlfriend can totally forget all the negotiating once we've made a choice. I'm sure you can find one or two personal experiences of your own to fit this situation.

So what's the point? We come to life from this wired box in which we live, the dimensions of which are defined by the array of decisions we have adopted as being necessary for our survival. Anything or any statement that is inconsistent with the operating principles of the box is automatically rejected as nonsense. I would be surprised if you have not thought that some of the material presented thus far falls into this category.

Therefore, to begin to gain mastery in life, we have to be willing to reconsider our long-held attitudes, opinions, and prejudices. To do so takes great courage, because it will possibly mean giving up our long-held survival mechanisms. It will appear as though we have made ourselves bare and vulnerable to the world. What, in fact, we will have done is to take that irreversible step through a door in which there is no return. Some call this process *transformation*.

One final point I would like to make before leaving this discussion is to emphasize the importance of the knowledge and skills we have accumulated. We literally couldn't make it in life from day to day without much of the knowledge we have acquired, whether based on true or imagined survival.

However, enough talk about theory; let's get down to some real life practical applications as we now venture into the complex world of relationship.

Chapter Seven

RELATIONSHIP

"Relationship means to be related, not in action, not in some project, not in an ideology — but to be totally united in the sense that the division . . . between individuals, between two human beings, does not exist at all at any level."

J. Krishnamurti

How We Put It Together

At the beginning of the second chapter I $_{...}$
which altered my perception of relationship. $_{...}$
simply the unconditional commitment to another pe$_{...}$
well-being. This is certainly a different way to de$_{...}$
you get some idea of what happens after having a realiza$_{...}$
life situations from an altered way of being. Before rejecting this vie$_{..}$
of hand, let's take a look at how I got to this point.

First of all, each of us has a fully developed reality of what a relationship is and how it should function in order to obtain desired results. Most of us have lived our lives out of this reality, consciously and unconsciously, expecting others to come around to adjusting to us. This was certainly true of me. Grudgingly, I discovered that a fundamental difficulty in being in relationship with another person is that, coming from my reality, the relationship works to the extent to which we see life in the same way. It's like having overlapping realities. When our realities do overlap, it is because the decisions we have made about relationships are similar.

To the extent that our realities do not overlap, there is conflict. Conflict is, of course, inevitable, since the probability of finding someone who sees the world exactly as I do is indeed low if not nil. We might represent this situation by Figure 4.

Therefore, in order to resolve the inherent conflicts, we need to have agreements. It's important to see that we all individually have a unique and complex network built about relationships. It is equally important to begin to realize that operating from this complex network, there can be no consistency in quality. Conflict must set in, because the basis of our artificially created realities about relationships has its genesis in survival, not love.

According to this model of relationship, the key to survival is separateness. The pinnacle of separateness is exclusive relationships. Relationships designed to exclude others are simply for survival and are ultimately nonsatisfying because this same view is applied to each other. Therefore, in exclusive relationships, we *unconsciously* begin to see our partners as threatening and something always happens to precipitate a conflict that drives us apart. If what I am suggesting sounds ludicrous, then note whether our relationships periodically and predictably have conflicts. The point here is not necessarily to prove these statements, but to begin to gain some insight into the consequences of operating from our reality of relationship.

Please note that I have not as yet said a word about the form external relationships should take! What I would like to develop are the consequences of operating from the viewpoint of controlling another individual. Sometimes there is closeness, followed by separation, which is caused by a major

55

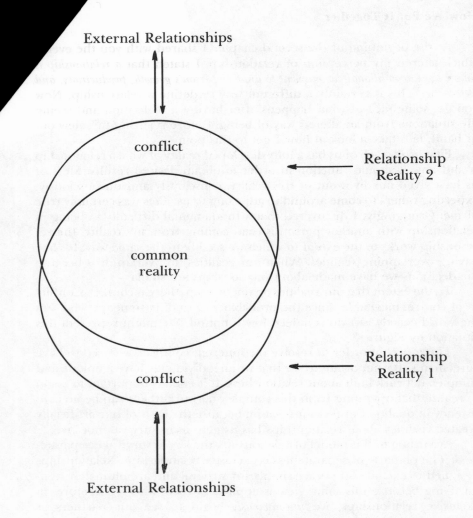

Figure 4 The dynamic nature of a conceptually derived relationship necessarily leads to conflict when the common reality is exceeded.

upset resulting from our nonoverlapping realities. I call this phenomenon the "accordion effect" in relationships, since life is about oscillating between the common and conflicting areas of the relationship. The driving mechanism is the preservation of our individual realities at all costs.

If we expand this view to external relationships, which are less intimate, then the extent of overlap of our realities is even less. Thus, we can more easily prevent conflict in these situations by avoidance.

Show Me the Way Out

The way out of this dilemma begins with awareness, acknowledgment, and evaluation of the system we individually constructed. Next, we need to give ourselves permission to move beyond the construction to provide the opportunity for a realization to occur. As long as we inflexibly hold on to our view of "how it should be," we will at least know that our relationships will not only consistently not work, but they can't work! If our beliefs are more important to us than the quality of our relationships, then there's nothing good or bad about this point of view. However, we must also be willing to claim responsibility for the results produced and not pretend to be victimized.

In one of our workshops, I had a question-and-answer session with one of the participants, in which she viewed her husband's relationship with his mother to be the source of their difficulties. In the course of the workshop, she discovered that the underlying issue for her was control of others in relationships. When she came face to face with the question, "Are you willing to give up control in order to have your relationships work?" she thought about it seriously and really became aware of this issue in a nonintellectual way for the first time. She replied, "No, I want to continue as I have always functioned, but now I am more willing to own the results. Perhaps I'll decide to change sometime in the future."

One of the most important relationships in my life is with my son, Danny. Until six years ago our relationship was ordinary. I was his dad and he was my son. I went out and earned the bread, and I thought he looked up to me as "master of the hearth." During that period he never told me what he really thought because he knew what was necessary for his own survival. "Humor the old man about how great he is!" After doing an extensive training, I discovered some things about me, which in turn allowed me to discover some things about him. We subsequently spent three weeks together with my telling him everything about me. That is, all the things I really didn't want him to know. Guess what? He knew all of them anyway! Not the details, but he knew the overall events.

This turned out to be a tremendous burden lifted from my shoulders.

57

I didn't have to pretend to be a great father anymore. I didn't have to hide or lie to him anymore (verbally and nonverbally). In fact, I often go to him for advice. Young people really see the world in a truthful and straightforward fashion. I discovered that most of the complications in my life could be reduced to a system of justifications based on my unwillingness to take responsibility for creating quality relationships.

Even though we operate in relationships out of our constructed realities, the fact is, no one's reality is better than anyone else's, since they are all survival based. The process that we probably consciously use for "falling in love" with someone comes almost totally from our concepts of what love is. Namely, characteristics of looks, size, hair, background, income, tenderness, understanding, wisdom, social status, recognition, etc. In effect, we fall in love with our individual realities of love, or as the song goes, "Falling in love with love is falling for make-believe." Fortunately, we do come to discover that the true source of relationship is beyond our concepts, but we still have difficulty in consistently escaping our self-imposed traps even when we want to.

Qualities of a Relationship That Works

If we examine very closely the way I described a relationship, after my realization, we can recognize two implications about it. One, it is independent of sex or age, and two, it is not defined in terms of the form it takes. That is, it does not prescribe what is done or not done as the definition of a relationship. For example, it makes no distinction between a love relationship, a platonic relationship, a friendly relationship, etc. These are based on what we do or don't do in relationship with another person. I reiterate, a relationship begins with an unconditional commitment to another person. The key word here is unconditional. How we individually express this unconditional commitment may not, and often does not, take the same form. Let me be more specific. There are qualities that I recognize when my relationship with a person or a group is really working.

One is timelessness. I totally lose track of time, which I assume to mean that I am fully present. That is, to the extent I am present with that person, there is really no past or future; there is only now. Haven't you noticed that when you are really having a great time with someone, time not only goes faster, but you can be less concerned about it? That's because you are really being present with that other person.

Another quality I notice is that I have no attention on me. I am really seeing the world through that other person's eyes, so to speak, and really understanding where they are coming from. I guess that's the quality of naturally being with another person.

A third quality is, I have no sense of judgment or evaluation of the other person or of what they are expressing. There is no conversation going on in my head such as, "I believe that, but not this," "Well, that makes sense, but the other point doesn't," etc. Essentially, there is an absence of viewing another person's sharing through my conditioning or reality.

I am sure there are other qualities that you have probably experienced in addition to those that I have mentioned. To begin to be aware of these qualities allows us to recognize clearly when our relationships are working well and what the sources might be when they are not. That is, to bring into our awareness new information to process so we may gain realizations about those aspects that consistently produce undesired results as well as desired results.

An Exercise or Two

Since realizations often begin with new awarenesses, here are two exercises you may want to try. Even though most of these exercises can be done mentally, I have found that the maximum benefit comes when they are actually done with pencil and paper. Perhaps when we write something, we are pinning ourselves down. In any case, make a list of expectations you know you require of another person in order to have a relationship work to your satisfaction. List these expectations in order of importance to you. Look over your list to make sure it is fairly complete.

There are a few suggestions for your consideration I'd like to make about the list. One, if you examine your list very carefully, you will discover that the sources of upsets, problems, and frustrations in your relationship can almost invariably be traced to an expectation you have of another person. The implication is, if the other person hasn't changed or is unlikely to change in the future, maybe an alternative is to reevaluate your expectations, since *you* are having the difficulty and probably not the other person.

Two, in large part many of our expectations are setups. What I am saying is that, for the most part, many of our expectations can't possibly be met by the other person in the way we have them visualized. After all, the expectation is in our minds. This routine actually goes a step further, we can now use the unfulfilled expectation as a way of gaining advantage of or one-upping our partners. If you have a partner who isn't too swift, this is an excellent routine to use. Not really!

Three, there appears to be some relationship between the length of a list of expectations and the number of quality relationships a person may have. In other words, the fewer expectations we have of other individuals, the more friends we tend to have and the higher the quality of the relationships.

Probably the most important use that can be made of your list is to share it with the person in question. It's surprising how many partners are totally unaware of what their mates expect. If you don't tell them directly, it's fair to assume they don't know. The same type of exchange might be done with personal friends, working relationships, etc.

I often make the statement that the quality of your life can be measured in terms of the quality of your relationships. Here's another exercise you might use to get a quantitative measure of the quality of your relationships and, correspondingly, of your life.

First, find yourself a quiet place where you will not be disturbed and where you feel very relaxed and clearheaded. Then, in sequence, mentally bring into your consciousness seven people whom you consider to be most important to you. Allow only one in at a time and give yourself a few minutes to consider the quality of your relationship in terms of communication, understanding, comfort level around that person, and the extent to which you mutually contribute to each other.

Then, fill in Table 2 by writing the seven names in the column labeled name. The second column is what is called the "importance factor." Some relationships (i.e., a mate), may be two or three times more important than others. Enter the factors appropriate to each for you. Then check a number for the quality rating. The last column is a number for each person, obtained by multiplying the "importance factor" by the "quality rating." The total of this column is listed as the present total.

If you are not satisfied with your present quality total, you might repeat the exercise, filling in what you feel would be an appropriate desired quality total you would like to have. Then, you might use the contents of this book to begin making the fundamental changes necessary to achieve your goal at some designated date in the future.

What's the Message?

The real message in this chapter is to have us begin to consider a relationship as an unconditional commitment to someone and to be aware that the instant it becomes conditional, we are consciously setting ourselves up for possible disappointment. Sometimes our expectations will be met and sometimes they won't, no matter how justified the expectation. Since all real relationships operate both with and without conditions, we now have a powerful tool at our disposal when our expectations are not met and conflict results: our list! We rush to our list and say, "I really wanted a number 5 and he (or she) didn't give it to me. He (or she) is the stimulus in the environment, and my expectation is the source of the upset." This is a statement of ownership; and it not only reduces the intensity of the conflict, but minimizes its time duration. Reducing the importance of our

60

RELATIONSHIP QUALITY RATING

NAME	IMPORTANCE FACTOR	1	2	3	4	5	6	7	8	9	10	TOTAL

Desired Total _____   Present Total _____

Table 2 A quantitative measure of the quality of life is an evaluation of our present relationships. The desired total is what we hope to have at some designated future date.

upsets to an unfulfilled expectation on a list allows us to discuss them within a framework where our conditioned behavioral patterns are clearly distinguishable from our inherent worth as human beings.

Coming from a natural way of being, which is a framework of unconditional love, means that any conflict which occurs in the practice of the relationship can simply be treated as an event within this framework, and is not equivalent to or of sufficient importance to invalidate or threaten the relationship. That is, for persons committed in relationship, be it personal or professional, no disagreement, upset, misunderstanding, unfulfilled expectation, etc., supersedes the relationship; in a manner of speaking, the relationship is sacrosanct.

There is probably no greater sense of insecurity in relationships than when one or more of the partners has a *feeling* that somehow, "I'm always walking on eggs," or trying desperately not to step on that inevitable land mine that will blow the relationship or partnership apart. When this sense exists, it's probably a waste of time to continue attempting to "solve" the never-ending sequence of problems that occurs, but to squarely confront the issue of commitment. This is particularly scary if it involves someone we love, respect, need for the success of a project, etc. Until we are prepared to deal with the possible loss of the person, we will remain an ineffective partner in the workability of that relationship, by choice! In fact, our role is that of a victim, hoping somehow that this feeling of noncommitment *inside* of us will somehow be solved *outside* of us.

The message here is that we have to be willing to tell the truth, at least to ourselves, about unworkable relationships in which we are presently involved. No real solution is possible without first locating the true source of the problem and that involves the scary and sometimes upsetting process of telling the truth about the matter. Only at this point are meaningful and permanent solutions possible.

Since we have begun discussing problems and upsets, let's take an in-depth look at how our understanding of these might be a source of valuable realizations and, correspondingly, resolutions.

Chapter Eight

PROBLEMS AND RELATED STRESS, AND RESOLUTIONS

*"The world that we have made
as a result of the level of thinking
we have done thus far,
creates problems that we cannot solve
at the level we created them."*

Albert Einstein

The True Source of Problems Can Be Deceptive

What is the relationship, if any, between problems and upsetting situations and realizations? That's really the point of this chapter. There are at least two responses that come to mind. Quite often, problems can be used to reveal a deeply hidden assumption we may have about similar-looking incidents that causes such problems to persist. Having the hidden assumption exposed for examination provides the opportunity for a permanent solution (a realization). With these thoughts in mind, let's develop in more detail a new and powerful skill in recognizing, analyzing, and solving problems and conflict. In the process, we will acquire a new awareness of the sources of stress and techniques for their reduction and management.

In the "Organizational Workshops" we hold, this discussion usually has a significant impact on the participants. Through self-discovery, they sometimes see for the first time that what we commonly identify as problems are not true problems at all. They are usually the circumstances and conditions produced by specific incidents that are symptomatic of the underlying problem. An analogy would be having a cold. A headache and coughing are symptoms of a cold, whereas the problem is the cold. We tend to concentrate our solutions around the prevailing circumstances and the resulting conditions. The reason the true problem is difficult to identify is not because we don't want to deal with it, but because it is so deeply unconscious and firmly based on commonly accepted assumptions.

What Is a Problem?

One way to view a problem is in terms of one of its common characteristics – persistence. A problem is always around. It's there in the morning when we awaken; it has breakfast with us, goes to work with us, and as soon as the appropriate situation arises, it springs into action, dragging us along. It instructs us how to react: whether to stuff it and experience the deeply suppressed type of stress or become violent and experience the extroverted form of stress.

Somehow, judging by the way I've developed this discussion thus far, having a problem sounds disturbingly victimizing. If we give some thought to it, we might well begin to see that we are quite often at effect when we either don't know how to or refuse to resolve problems. We just can't seem to shake this issue of responsibility, can we? Before getting into solutions just yet, let's really expose the intricate network we've individually put together, which consistently produces undesired results called problems.

For something to persist, there is usually a stalemate. That would seem to imply two equally opposing points of view. When analyzed in detail by a skillful person who strips aside the emotions and interpretations, there usually appears to be some inconsistency or some justification that is not valid. It is the identification of this inconsistency that initiates the process of discovering the real source of the problem. We'll illustrate this process with an example for greater clarity.

One of the more common problems that comes up for discussion in the workshops for organizations is, "I don't know what my job responsibilities are." In my attempt to assist the participant in discovering a new insight about this issue, I usually focus on the individual's willingness to precipitate the action that resolves the problem. Therefore, my initial approach is to avoid dealing with questions like, "Have you been given a job description?" "Can you communicate with your boss to find out?" "What do you think your responsibilities are?" etc. These are probably all important questions at some point, but initially I attempt to have the participant discover the source of their apparent disability.

In a specific workshop, the process between a participant and the workshop leader went like this: Workshop leader: "What do you stand to gain by not knowing your job responsibilities?" Participant: "Nothing." Workshop leader: "Since there are apparently no "real" payoffs for you, make up some possible reasons that don't apply to you." Participant: "Well, let's see, my time is my own; I can't be held accountable for what I produce or don't produce." (The participant started becoming uneasy at this point, suspecting that she had been "tricked" into saying something better left unsaid, which was true!) Workshop leader: "Is there anything else you can think of that someone else might gain by not knowing their job responsibilities?" Participant: After considering the question for what seemed like an eternity (one minute to be accurate), she said, "Every time I finish something, no one approves of it anyway!"

Afterwards she just sat there trying to discover where that statement had come from. It had apparently slipped out inadvertently. The implications for her were overwhelming. She shared that she could immediately see this happening throughout her life and she had never been aware of it from this point of view. She always knew somehow that people wouldn't approve totally of what she produced, so she had decided long ago that it simply wasn't worth trying. But to think that this hidden assumption was the possible source of her not taking responsibility to find out what her job responsibilities were was so remote she would have never connected them.

Once the justification or hidden assumption is *realized* by the participant, the problem is essentially solved. At this point, very few people need to be instructed in terms of techniques to approach their boss or how to communicate with their boss, since the true barrier had nothing to do with the boss in the first place.

In some cases the participant does not have a realization about the exposed assumption, he simply sees it as an intellectual discovery that has moved from unaware unaware to the aware unaware circle (Chapter 1). The difference for this individual is that he has been "brought to the water," and, as such, *chooses* not to drink. However, he can no longer pretend to be victimized by his problem since he is actually choosing that situation and all of its undesirable consequences in preference to acknowledging the truthful application of the hidden assumption to himself.

Another characteristic associated with problems is disablement or the need for help. Associated victimizing statements are "I can't," "I am unable," "What would they think?" etc. Generally, cause and solution are outside of the person. The area of disablement can be analyzed in the following way:

On the surface there is a	STATEMENT of the Problem
Beneath the Statement, there is a	REACTION (emotion, unconsciousness, etc.)
Beneath the Reaction, there is a	JUSTIFICATION (usually invalid)
Which, when exposed by the	TRUTHFUL ACKNOWLEDGMENT of that which is apparently damaging to reveal,
Leads to the	REALIZATION
and ownership of	RESPONSIBILITY

Analysis of a Problem

A perfect example of the analysis above is the one I described about myself and my office staff in Chapter 5. Let's illustrate this process again, using the diagram in Figure 5 with another example from one of the workshops.

The first thing we notice about the diagram is the description of the situations, above the surface, that were considered to be a series of different problems involving a junior-level manager named Jim. In the workshop exercise, Jim chose insufficient salary as the description of his problem in the organization. What follows is a condensed approximate reproduction of the workshop dialogue and description:

Questioner: What's your problem, Jim?
Jim: I'm not being paid enough and I'm unhappy.

67

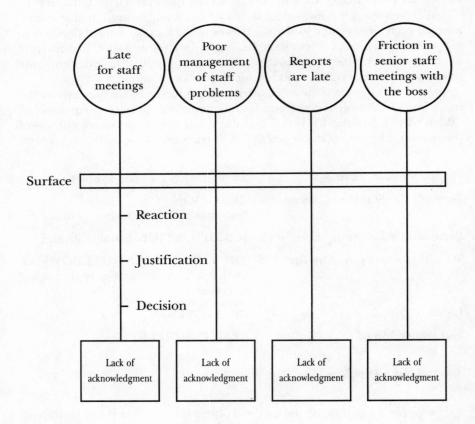

Figure 5 Symptoms of problems (above the surface) sourced by the real unconscious underlying problem. "People show how much they appreciate you by how much they acknowledge you."

68

Questioner: How much would you need to earn to be happy?
Jim: I don't know exactly.

Questioner: Why don't you quit and get another job?
Jim: I like my work.

Questioner: Then is money really the problem?
Jim: (Reaction of surprise) Money is important! (Complete narrative on money and wanted to know if the Questioner thought money to be important.)

Questioner: Is money really the problem?
Jim: (Pause) I guess not.

Questioner: Then what do you think the real problem is?
Jim: (Confusion) People show how much they appreciate you by how much they pay you.

Questioner: Is the issue acknowledgment of your contributions as a manager?
Jim: (Pause) I guess so, maybe.

Questioner: Why don't you tell your boss?
Jim: He should know, I shouldn't have to tell him.

Questioner: So, you can continue to be unhappy, complain to the other employees that he's not paying you adequately, and thus undermine the organization? Is that your intent?
Jim: Obviously not!

Questioner: Well, that is what's happening, isn't it?
Jim: Well, yes, but it's not my fault.

Questioner: Are you willing to tell him?
Jim: I don't know.

Questioner: Then are you willing to be responsible for the consequences of not telling him? Things remain as they are, and you really have nothing to complain about with your newly discovered insight.
Jim: (Long pause) I'll tell him tomorrow. You know, I feel a load lifted from my shoulders.

Although most of this example is self-explanatory, there are a few important points to emphasize. We normally resolve problem situations above the surface that appear to be different, but they typically have a common source. As you can see, this is the reason we have never run out of problems; neither will we do so in the future. For those of you who have always known this fact, you have also probably experienced people's

69

reactions when their statement of the problem is challenged. These range from anger and self-righteousness to "How dare you not accept everything I say."

Going beyond his reaction and justification, Jim discovered his "hidden assumption" neatly packaged as "appreciation is shown by acknowledgment." His unconscious reaction to lack of acknowledgment was "I don't perform." This, I suspect, was also the point at which he had the realization that his hidden assumption was not necessarily true. He probably *was* appreciated and the manner in which his boss acknowledged him was not a communication that Jim received. In a sense, such a request can never be fully met, since only Jim knows for sure in what form and how often his expected acknowledgment is sufficient. This problem, of clear communication between co-workers and colleagues, is one we will discuss at length in the next chapter.

The difficulties we have in discovering and owning our "hidden assumptions" are there because they have served us well for so long and they make good sense! In examining the two cases we have discussed in this chapter, both, taken as isolated statements, appear to be perfectly reasonable. So having a realization requires us to literally go beyond the "reasonable level of thinking" in which we operate day to day. A reasonable question might be, "Why would Jim have such difficulty in exposing such an illogical assumption?" The assumption was probably adopted at a very young age and until the workshop, much of Jim's life was probably about collecting evidence to prove the validity of the hidden assumption. Jim had what appeared to be a substantial investment in his assumption.

It is important to note that the Questioner (who was skilled) could have had a long discussion with Jim about salary or some other diversionary subject, solving that particular issue temporarily, but not the true underlying problem.

I would also like to point out that it typically doesn't matter what conflicting situation (above the surface) is chosen, the process usually leads to the real underlying problem. In other words, a problem with a common source shows up in many guises as illustrated in Figure 5. In the course of the process, if someone consciously or unconsciously senses you are getting close to the "contents of the box," be prepared for a variety of evasive actions. I assure you, protecting the contents of the box from revelation is vital. Even when the contents are revealed, and the person is asked, "Are you willing to give up that which is obviously not true?" it is not unusual for the reply to be, "I'll think about it," or just plain "No."

In one of the university student workshops, a participant named Janet stated that she was having a problem with her father, who always insisted that she should clean her room daily. Janet had lived away from home and had only recently moved back. Therefore, she found the adjustment difficult, having been independent and having adopted her own personal domestic life-style.

Janet indicated that it was very difficult for her to talk about this situation because she would "cry and get angry." She stated that such emotional displays were the same as a "loss of control." Janet continued, "When I cry, I become vulnerable. When I become vulnerable, I stand to be hurt emotionally. When I get hurt, I feel rejected."

The final statement that she made, which appeared to surprise her the instant she shared it was, "When someone rejects you, they don't love you." She just sat there studying that statement for a minute or so. When something similar to this has happened to me, the feeling I get is like having the statement "slip out" without being properly censored by my mind.

You can probably see the stepwise problem-solving process Janet went through by examining the quoted expressions, which culminated with the boxed statement connecting rejection to being unloved. At this point (having had the realization), Janet's problem is essentially solved as far as any outside assistance is concerned. The realignment of her behavior with the extent of invalidity of the boxed statement is a process she began to undertake at a rate of her own choosing. We might also note that Janet went through several justifying statements (Figure 5), vulnerable to emotionally hurt to rejected, before getting to the bottom line.

Finally, Janet shared that the technique she had used, in order to avoid losing control, was to take on behavioral patterns indicative of the following expressions: "Be the leader," "Be the director," "Don't cry," and "Be strong." You might guess that experiencing life from these perspectives would inevitably and consistently lead to "above the surface" problems. Until this exercise, Janet had unconsciously decided that it was more important to *have* these problems rather than bring up her boxed statement for examination. Therefore, in spite of the fact that people will say, "I really don't want these [above the surface] problems," what they are unconsciously saying is that "I prefer having these undesirable problems rather than going through the process of discovering a more important underlying motive I choose not to have exposed."

There is another vitally important point to be made here and one I have consistently observed in high school and college workshops: *the major preoccupation of these young people is whether their parents truly love them.* No matter what the subject of the workshop may be at any given time, for example, "adjusting to a demanding teacher," the deeply hidden underlying question, which may actually be disabling to a student in terms of performance is, "Do my parents really love me?" One student had the two related by the assumption, "Any adult who demands anything is confirming that they don't love me." Unless you've been through this experience personally, this concluding fear might appear to be somewhat far-fetched. But, give it serious thought; simply consider this question over a week or so, without rejecting it out of hand.

I want to emphasize that I know of no unique technique which works all the time. These were specific cases from our workshops. Keeping in mind the overall approach we use and the fact that the initial statement of the problem that people suggest is usually not it, but is a starting point, you can devise your own technique appropriate to your personal situation. Remember, however, we are all very new at solving problems at this level, so we must exercise care, understanding, and empathy and realize it will be a slow learning process.

The other point I should add is that in given situations, it may be perfectly appropriate to resolve an issue at the level above the surface. It is obviously not necessary or practical to solve all of our problems at the level I've described above.

What's the Connection Between Upsetting Problems and Stress?

Up to this point we have concentrated mainly on those aspects of our well-being involving the manner in which we psychologically react to external stimuli. I am also aware that a delicate, dynamic balance exists between the psychological and the physical aspects of our being. Thus, I would like to emphasize that our psychological well-being is equally dependent on our physical fitness.

Within this framework, we recognize that excessive stress can result from certain types of problems that are upsetting; where we view an upset as a special type of recurring problem which occurs suddenly. Generally, an upset has some, but not necessarily all, of the following qualities associated with it:

1. An unfulfilled expectation.

2. An unaccomplished intention.

3. An undelivered communication.

4. Loss of closeness with someone or something.

5. Reduction or complete loss of communication. (Sometimes even physical separation).

6. Cessation of participation.

Now it gets really tough to swallow these if you've only recently attempted this type of self-examination.

72

7. Notice that this isn't the first time you've seen this incident – perhaps with different people, in a different setting, etc., but essentially the script is the same.

8. Somehow, we always return to the same bottom line, an attempt to escape being responsible for something. On a first reading, this statement may seem rather remote. If such is the case, I invite you to simply consider it for a couple of weeks.

Hans Selye[6] has defined stress as the nonspecific response of the body to any demand made upon it. It may equally well be viewed as the physical response to imagined and real threats to our survival. Distress is more often used to connote that form of excessive stress resulting principally from imagined threats. Therefore, our bodies are placed in the well-known "fight or flight" state. So, if there is no real threat, we are stuck in this heightened form of physical readiness with nothing to play out.

For primitive man, in a world of real physical dangers, the stress response was immensely useful for his survival. For modern man, it is much less so; and many of the dangers we perceive are strictly imagined.

If physical release through exercise is not readily available, then our minds follow through with the imagined threat as though it were real. We begin to devise scenarios and make up stories about the situation that produced the stress reaction and, worst of all, we devise a strategy for "defending ourselves."

The situation which comes to mind are the endless wasted hours that employees of organizations devote to strategies and counter-strategies in order to protect themselves and their domains. In most cases, there is actually nothing to protect and the time and energy devoted to this activity is simply not worth the price we pay in terms of distress. For example, we commonly react to disagreement and criticism in the same way we do to actual physical threats to our survival. The body's automatic reaction to threat, as instructed by the mind, is the same as it would be for a physical attack. Depending on the extent of our imaginative survival mode, we may conclude that someone or some group is out to "get us." The key to our healthy adjustment and well-being is to gain the ability to distinguish between real and imaginary threats to our survival.

Stress Management Through Problem Resolution

Since problems and upsets are clearly major sources of the day-to-day excessive stress in our lives, we now have new insights into reducing possible harmful effects. In addition to the traditional techniques such as exercise,

73

hobbies, diet, adequate rest, etc., we can also devise strategies to address problems and upsetting situations. First, we can begin to recognize, with greater clarity, that many of the situational conflicts we encounter are probably symptoms of an underlying assumption or presupposition that we have been previously unaware of. In fact, we might start to keep a private diary of incidents that have resulted in conflict, with very brief entries such as:

What upset me?
What happened (without interpretation)?
How could I have avoided it?
Have similar conflicts occurred previously?

After a couple weeks of this written exercise you will begin to gain valuable insights about yourself. Based upon the data compiled from the written exercise you can begin experimenting with various personally created coping mechanisms, until you find one or a combination that works best. I must hasten to add that a coping mechanism is a temporary solution to the conflicting condition that occurs above the surface, and it must be revised regularly, since the form of each incident varies. This may indeed be a reasonable approach to many of our less important problems in life.

On the other hand, there appears to be at least two major areas of life that most people choose to handle at a more fundamental level of resolution. Those are work and personal and/or home life, since they typically dominate so much of our lives. This is basically the process of discovering our individual "hidden assumptions." To assist someone in discovering a hidden assumption is all that anyone can do for someone else. At that point, the problem is solved and a decision must be made. As I previously stated, the individual has essentially been brought to the water to either "drink" or "not drink." In either case, the situation will never be the same again. To drink is to resolve the issue permanently. Not to drink reduces the previous martyr and victim role to fraud and deception.

Depending on the nature of an individual's medical history, a licensed therapist may be the appropriate choice. In many situations, however, this procedure is successfully accomplished in workshops, support groups, with personal friends, and occasionally alone by persons with unusual self-discipline. However, I would never try to outsmart my mind anymore, by assuming that I have unusual self-discipline; it has fooled me too many times! People who typically say, "I thought it over and the situation is really clear to me now . . ." are more often than not fooling themselves and ultimately come up with self-serving answers or solutions. There is one other important point to remember in assisting someone in clarifying a problem or a conflict that I would like to emphasize. In general, we find that it is extremely difficult to assist an individual in solving any problem that we have not solved for ourselves. Typically, both individuals get lost in a hopeless process.

Now we will integrate a number of the subjects discussed thus far into one – communication; the essence of which is to have our intent known.

Chapter Nine

COMMUNICATION WITH INTENT

"I know that you believe that you understand what you think I said, but I am not sure you realize that what you heard is not what I meant."

Anonymous

What Was That I Said?

I had always thought that communication was somehow embodied in what I said, how I said it, and the apparent impact what I said had on those listening. You might say that I had a system that was similar to most models describing the process of communication.

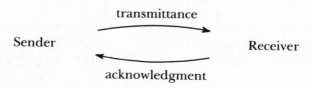

That is, someone transmits a communication to a person or group, who in turn acknowledges in some form that something was indeed transmitted. Based on this feedback, the sender then becomes the receiver and the process is reversed. The true embodiment of communication, however, is involved with the subtleties at several levels that are removed from the obvious transmittance. These levels of conscious and unconscious communication will be discussed in turn.

In order to be successful at getting what I wanted, I would adjust the three variables mentioned above to fit the situation or the person. Sometimes the approach I used worked and sometimes it didn't. When it didn't, I knew that what I should have used was a No. 6; instead I used a No. 5. Oh well, I just missed it by one number. I'll know better next time.

You might remember I stated in Chapter 5 that one way to become aware of what we intend is to simply observe what is produced as a result of our action. In the process of using this approach in a number of situations, I had one of my "aha's" again in the area of communication. *Communication is an expression of intent.* Specifically, what I truly intend, whether conscious or unconscious to me, is what gets communicated. In this sense, the communication is not only solely dependent on me, but the result produced does not validate or invalidate my intent. That is, if my communication is oranges, and you receive apples, this in no way means that I did not truly intend oranges, whether you received oranges or not. I refer to this exchange as a miscommunication. Most of the time the result that is generated is consistent with my desired conscious or unconscious objective. What often eludes us is the fact that we are unaware and unconscious of objectives in communication, which have overriding importance relative to those objectives we consciously profess.

An example of such an unconscious communication is the one I discussed previously about maintaining control over my staff. When one of

79

them would submit a report to me for consideration, the usual form of my sincere reply was, "You did an excellent job on that report, now all it needs are a 'few' adjustments from me and we'll be ready to submit it." The real communication here is, "It's never good enough until I've expressed it in the 'right' way (my way!)." Now, the way I handle reports that fall short of what I judge to be of an expected quality is to either state or write what I think the expectation is and have the staff upgrade the quality. This approach not only acknowledges them as being fully functional, but it also assists them in their professional development. My overall objective with the staff, during the time period I work with them as a manager, is to have them go away in better shape than when they started, both personally and professionally.

Another example of an unconscious intent having greater importance than the verbal message occurred in one of the workshops. It involved a father attempting to influence his teen-age daughter's attitude toward having a tidy room and being generally more sensitive to the tidiness of their home. This issue was only one of several that had polarized their relationship in general. After several "nice" attempts to persuade her with no success, the action he decided upon was from the standpoint of "man of the house." His verbal communication to his daughter was a stern order to "clean your room because I said so!" This approach was successful in having her clean her room, but only when ordered to do so. In his examination of this communication, he professed that his objective was to have her learn habits of domestic tidiness whether she preferred to learn or not. He considered this action his responsibility as a parent. What she probably heard was "as man of the house, you do what I say, whether you like it or not." *If* the latter statement was indeed the one received by his daughter, I suggested that it may have unconsciously been of overriding importance to him also. After considering his daughter's reaction and my suggestion, he was not sure which of the two he had truly intended; to exercise his authority as a father or to have her learn desirable domestic habits. He shared that his daughter had probably assumed the former and concluded, "This is more evidence that he really doesn't love me." Thus, this episode did not serve to enhance their relationship. He won the battle and continued to lose the war.

As a father who has encountered this exact situation with my teen-age son, I know how initially ridiculous the father's unconscious motives that I suggested may appear. Initially, in using an "understanding" approach of my own, I proposed to my son that we tidy his room together. It ultimately got to the point where he was observing me clean his room. At this point I decided the solution to this problem was to simply close his door and not allow the condition of his room to spill over into the rest of the house. It

80

was only after this attempted solution to *his* problem that I realized that he didn't have a problem at all! I had the problem! Then it dawned on me that maybe this was one of those problems that didn't require solving by some different course of action, but to simply share with him what was going on inside of me whenever I saw his untidy room – or for that matter, untidiness anywhere! I remember after one of our discussions, Danny said, "Dad, you look relieved."

I am not certain anything was solved. However, I do know for certain that I don't react in the same way I used to and sometimes he does clean his room. I still do not approve of his room being in a state of disarray for several days, but I do approve of him as a person, and he is clear about this distinction.

I am convinced that the resolution to miscommunication between parents and children is based on the necessity to establish a supportive relationship *first*. It is only through relationship that we begin to truly listen to what others are intending, irrespective of their verbal statements. Therefore, the key to initiating meaningful dialogue in a number of typical teenage problem areas, i.e., tidiness, academic performance, drugs, etc., begins with the willingness to be in relationship with children; relationship in the sense we have discussed in Chapter 6.

A popular example of the same type of unconscious communication occurs in intimate relationships. There are various versions of this routine, but it comes packaged as "clubbing someone over the head with the truth." We commonly use anger as a lead-in to tell someone the truth that we have suppressed for some time. What, in fact, we are truly communicating are our frustration and our anger to someone, usually based on the assumption that under normal circumstances it is unsafe to communicate clearly. In some situations I can imagine it may indeed be unsafe; but for the majority of us, the unstated statement is, "I hold you responsible for my inability to communicate naturally with you." Notice, the instant responsibility is outside of us; we are disabled. The statement that empowers the individual, regardless of the action taken, is, "I am responsible for my unwillingness to communicate naturally with you because . . ." (Fill in your own reason.)

From a practical point of view, I simply observe what I have produced as a result of my communication, and it is practically always consistent with my true intent. Sometimes it takes a little practice in truth-telling to get to the point where we start to discover whether winning *sometimes* in relationships is more important than "apparently losing" and winning *all the time*! What I'm saying is that sometimes accepting the truth about our behavior brings up feelings of guilt, being wrong, being bad, which are associated with losing. Whereas, self-acceptance by acknowledging the truth about ourselves provides the key to gaining valuable insights that were previously unavailable. *The insight comes only after the realization of the truth about ourselves.*

Notice the implications involved in viewing communication in this manner. It suggests that we are actually communicating all the time, both verbally and nonverbally – which I'm sure is no surprise. It also suggests that communication is occurring at a level which is even more subtle than nonverbal. That is, the expression of our intent is quite often unconscious and unaware *to us*; it is what I call, in this case, subliminal.

Subliminal Communication

What the previous examples have in common is that the underlying intent, in all three cases, was not only unconscious, but also unaware. That is, prior to our insight about that which we truly intend, we are unconscious *and* unaware of our true intention. Therefore, intention, in this sense, implies more than what we unconsciously have in mind to do or to bring about. This realization suggests an even more subtle level of nonverbal communication than is normally considered in most models; and, it is of overriding importance. I refer to this level or type of communication as *subliminal*, that communication which occurs outside of the domain of conscious awareness.

According to this view, communication is either conscious or unconscious, as diagrammed below.

Conscious Awareness (verbal and nonverbal)

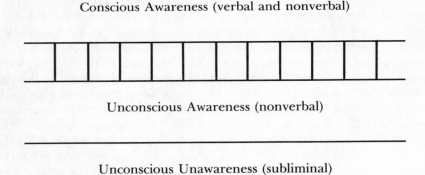

Unconscious Awareness (nonverbal)

Unconscious Unawareness (subliminal)

Conscious awareness is that which is communicated directly and explicitly; i.e., talking, touching (to communicate something), gestures, body language, facial expressions, etc. The transmission at this level is simply the content of the message, of which the sender and the receiver are both consciously aware. It may be a request or a statement in verbal or nonverbal form.

82

Unconscious awareness is that which is knowingly communicated unconsciously (by habit), such as emotions and the nature of a relationship; i.e., anger, fear, sadness, joy, etc. An example is a person who unconsciously (by habit) intimidates people when she (he) communicates. She (he) is aware of this behavior and does it unconsciously. An analogy would be the unconscious process of driving to work each morning. We don't consciously say, "I will drive to Third South, turn left, and proceed on State Street until I reach the watershed, etc." Through repetition and habit, we drive to work each morning unconsciously aware of where we intend to go.

Unconscious unawareness is that which is unknowingly communicated unconsciously. It is truly the expression of what we intend to result from delivering a communication. This level of communication supersedes the two discussed above in terms of importance. With rare exception, what happens is what I intend. Examples are control, superiority, domination, etc. A communication indicative of this level is, "My intent is to maintain control of my staff by inducing fear in them (in order to protect myself). It is important to understand that the individual is unconscious and unaware of this way of being and is therefore unable to do anything about it as a conscious act. If such a way of being is brought to his (her) attention, it then moves to one or the other two levels, depending on how seriously he (she) considers it to be. If such consideration initiates an internal process, then a realization ultimately occurs, and the survival-based way of being is permanently handled. Notice the analogy of this level of communication to the realm of "unaware unaware" discussed in Chapter 1 and the hidden assumption in problem solving discussed in Chapter 8.

In order to illustrate further this way of viewing communication, we might consider a series of examples:

GOSSIP AND RUMOR AT THE WORKSITE

Conscious Awareness (content)
"I heard that Bill's presentation was a disaster."

Unconscious Awareness (emotional tone)
"I am 'unconsciously aware' that spreading or repeating gossip is 'covertly hostile' as an emotional tone."

Unconscious Unawareness (intent)
"I am 'unconsciously unaware' that my intent is to undermine or destroy his reputation." (It never occurred to me, and now that I know, it will no longer be my intent.)

It is important to recognize that all three statements are communicated simultaneously. This is also true of the following examples.

PERSONAL RELATIONSHIP

Man to Woman

Conscious Awareness (content verbal statement)
"I am sorry that I didn't get a chance to call you last weekend to let you know that I had a previous engagement."

Unconscious Awareness
"I just wanted you to know that I am serious about the potential of this relationship." (Interest)

Unconscious Unawareness
"I have a pattern of cautiously entering into relationships because I always ultimately get rejected."

Woman to Man (Response)

Conscious Awareness (above verbal statement received)
"I have no expectations of you in this relationship. You don't have to tell me everything you do."

Unconscious Awareness
"What 'I' am really saying is that I don't want you to have expectations of me." (Conservatism)

Unconscious Unawareness
"What I am unconsciously and unawaredly saying is that I am unwilling to be committed to this relationship" (or maybe any that might potentially be intimate and workable).

HOSPITAL SITUATION

Doctor's Communication to a Nurse

Conscious Awareness (content)
"Nurse, can you handle the clean-up procedure on this patient?"

84

Unconscious Awareness (emotional tone)
    "I hope you can handle this menial task." (Condescending)

Unconscious Unawareness (intent)
    "I am a superior human being, relative to you!"

Nurse's Communication to the Doctor

Conscious Awareness (receives the content statement from above).
    "Yes, Doctor, I can."

Unconscious Awareness
    "You think you are so smart." (Covert hostility)

Unconscious Unawareness
    "I am/am not inferior!"

If inferior/superior is an issue for the nurse, there is the reaction indicated above by his (male nurse) response to the (female) doctor's statement and he goes away feeling less in terms of self-esteem.

If inferior/superior is not an issue for the nurse, then he receives the communication from the doctor and is unaffected by it.

If inferior/superior is not an issue for either of them, then the entire communication occurs at the conscious awareness level.

OFFICE BEHAVIOR

Boss to Worker

Conscious Awareness
    "Fred, I didn't think it was appropriate, according to rank, for you to discuss a proposal with another section without my clearance."

Unconscious Awareness
    "I am unconsciously aware that I intimidate and threaten my employees to keep them in line." (Intimidation)

Unconscious Unawareness
    "My intent is to control and dominate those I am in relationship with."

Worker to Boss

Conscious Awareness (content statement received from above)
    "I'm sorry, Larry. I didn't think it was necessary to check every conversation I have with you."

85

Unconscious Awareness
"I have no intention of checking with you before talking to anyone I please." (Antagonism)

Unconscious Unawareness
"I will not be controlled or dominated by you (or anyone)."

We can now begin to gain an appreciation for the overriding importance of the context within which communication occurs. It truly is about where we are coming from and provides the basis of our intent.

It's About Where We're Coming From!

Probably the most important part of the communication process is initiated before we say or do anything, that is, by our way of being. One of the clearest examples that comes to mind is the science seminars that a colleague and I have presented for some years to grade-school students. The first five minutes in front of them is probably one of the most nervous times I can remember, because there is no technique or method that works on them. They demand the real thing or nothing. I distinctly recall all of my mental messages, such as "win them over," "get them on your side," "make them laugh," etc., in order to have some typical feedback that I was communicating. When it finally dawned on me that I might simply try being natural and talk to them as capable and equal individuals, something happened. The entire atmosphere of the presentation instantly changed from one of my reacting to what I perceived to be their reaction to me, to one of no expectations and freedom to allow the presentation to evolve spontaneously.

They laughed when I didn't intend to be funny and were serious when I did. The most difficult adjustment for me was to their natural mannerisms. As I made my part of the presentation, some kids looked out of a window, a few had conversations of their own, some made it obvious that they were clearly unimpressed by the preliminaries and wanted to get on with the demonstrations. As long as one person appeared to be interested, I was committed to enjoying myself, and I did.

I learned from those experiences that the most important aspect of having verbal information clearly communicated is the context in which it is delivered. That is, the atmosphere or the framework always dictates the nature of that which is communicated; and the content is essentially used to express our intent. This is true of all communication, irrespective of whether it is a board meeting, a religious meeting, a lecture, or a one-on-one sharing between friends. It's about where we're coming from. Our intent can be one that is supportive and nurturing or one that is not.

I Never Thought About Gossip in That Way!

One of the most counterproductive ways in which we unconsciously communicate is through gossip and rumor. Essentially, gossiping is the act of retelling and/or fabricating stories, especially about the private affairs of others. Gossip is so commonplace that we are generally unaware of how often we participate in it either spreading gossip or receiving gossip. These stories are, however, seldom told to the person being gossiped about.

The results, in terms of the person gossiped about, are generally a reduced opinion, generated suspicion, and an altered form of relationship with that person in the future. There is never a positive intent to come from gossip; neither is there ever a positive result. It is vital to understand that there are no innocent participants in the gossiping process; i.e., the gossiper or the receiver of gossip. The ultimate result of gossip is to undermine interpersonal relationships and, ultimately, the efficient operation of organizations. If we were to reduce the fraction of gossip by half at our workplace, the quality of relationships would increase by a corresponding fraction. From our experience in workshops, this module presentation to organizations or businesses usually has the most immediate positive effect on the interpersonal operation.

You're probably saying by now, "How do 'I,' as a single employee, reduce the gossip at my job?" The first step is to now simply be *aware* when you are participating in the process, i.e., either receiving or spreading gossip. Recounts about others which are enhancing are not considered to be gossip. Second, consider the necessity of the communication and the effect it would have if said about you. Third, you must ultimately ask, "What is truly my intent?"

There are no hard-and-fast rules in the solution to this form of communication. Reducing its counterproductive effects in the workplace or our private lives is another process we can now begin to learn and, as a result, develop a procedure unique to our own personal styles. This process typically initiates a shift in the way we judge and view others and provides a basis for an expanded willingness to be more accepting.

Does Accepting Others Have Anything to Do with Me?

In order to communicate naturally, we have to be willing to establish a relationship. We start by learning how to simply be with someone. Initially,

87

one of the most difficult workshop exercises is for the participants to pair off and simply be with another person with *no conversation*. The silence is deafening. One way to begin this process is to notice our level of discomfort around certain people. Then, simply turn up the volume of the conversation going on in our heads so that we might hear how we judge, evaluate, and categorize them. Again, awareness is the first step.

Second, we might want to begin questioning whether what we see through our filtered vision is more our own construction than the truth about someone else. During this phase of questioning, there may be not only resistance in our minds but also physical sensations in our bodies. This resistance is sometimes referred to as a barrier to communication. The approach I use when barriers occur is to simply do nothing but be aware of them and see how much resistance I am willing to give up. Reducing our resistance is accomplished by our willingness to acknowledge the truth about our thoughts. Ultimately, the only person who knows this truth is you.

When we allow ourselves to be truthful about our thoughts, the barriers to natural communication begin to fall and we become more accepting of others. In this stepwise process, so far we haven't said one word about verbalizing anything. The essence of natural communication is to simply be with someone without any mental activity about ourselves.

This process reminds me of the Native American saying, "Oh Great Spirit, grant that I may not criticize my neighbor until I have walked a mile in his moccasins."

A few years ago I had the opportunity to go through this stepwise process I have just described with a woman who was overweight. As I sat across from her, the first thought I had was that they had paired me with the wrong person, particularly since I had missed the attractive woman next to us by one chair. Then I began to notice the discomfort and negative attitude I had about overweight people, represented by Judy. The exercise involved our sharing with each other thoughts and attitudes that appeared to get in the way of our being natural in conversation. I was very relieved that these exercises had not gotten to the point where other people could read my mind.

After sharing with Judy some nonsense in an attempt to avoid the issue, she asked me why was I lying? She did so in a nonthreatening and understanding way, as if *I was having a problem*! Finally, I shared with her that the bottom line was I had the opinion that people were overweight because they chose to be and that most of them had a lot of justifications around the issue, which sounded to me like they were being victims. Furthermore, it also appeared that overweight people did not want to claim ownership of their body, particularly what I considered to be their undesirable excess.

The more we systematically went through the exercise, the more I could begin to see something I had never realized before. All the thoughts at the surface I had about overweight people, such as unattractive, slow-thinking, burdensome, etc., were camouflaging the real button, which was "since overweight people chose to be overweight, they also chose not to be responsible." Irresponsibility and victims drive me up the wall.

What's the value of the example I have just described? I discovered that we don't have to be overweight in order for this issue to play a significant role in our relationships. That is, if I consider the condition of overweight to be undesirable, then my system of beliefs is automatically activated before, during, and after my interpersonal interaction with an individual I consider to be overweight. In this sense, it is an issue for me that sets severe limitations on my relationship with people I consider to be overweight. Furthermore, the reaction I have to overweight people is not caused by them; they only serve to activate my system of beliefs. Thus, the solution to my working with/around and being friends with overweight people lies in my willingness to deal with me, rather than requiring that they necessarily change as a condition for natural relationship and communication. Anyway, the only person I can change with surety is me.

Finally, Judy assisted me in discovering that the real issue was not about being overweight, but about my strongly held beliefs centered on responsibility and victims. This realization provided me the insight to more clearly distinguish between the reality of an individual's condition of overweight and my thoughts of abdication of responsibility. In retrospect, I think this exercise provided the opportunity for me to see that basically *what I am unwilling to accept about other people is what I am unwilling to acknowledge to be true about myself.* Judy simply served as a mirror.

Communication with Intent

Up to this point, most of the discussion has focused on communication that we normally engage in. Let's take a look at communicating naturally. One way to view communication as being natural is the open sharing of feelings, emotions, thoughts, and information and the willingness to simply be with someone. It also involves the acceptance of others, not like it's forced upon us, but really having them be okay exactly the way they are. Until this level is reached, there will always be some impediment to communicating.

Ultimately, communication is about sharing. Sharing implies a certain quality of love, care, and affection. It involves a trust between individuals, where they know that it's safe to express themselves without judgment and evaluation. In fact, there is total support in discovering together how it

89

actually is, rather than the "should be's," "ought to be's," etc.

In order to have this level of sharing, we must be free to observe and to listen. This type of freedom must be created, not by doing something, but by the willingness to confront those barriers which automatically appear in the process of living.

Having the willingness to confront the major barriers that prevent us from excelling and achieving our goals is really the challenge that stands between us and an expanded quality of living; irrespective of whether these barriers involve relationships, problems, or communication. For those of you who are willing to accept this challenge, I dedicate the final chapter to you — to "those who chase stars."

Chapter Ten

FOR THOSE WHO CHASE STARS

"Those who are really committed to an activity come to it and live it naturally, not out of coercion, necessity, or gratification. Their very being is a moment-by-moment expression of it, with no greater preoccupation. To expect or require commitment of another is to cause conflict and confusion. Alternatively, providing the opportunity for examination and choice is the key to resolving commitment and noncommitment."

The Author

What's a Star-Chaser?

This chapter is dedicated to *those who chase stars*; to those who find excelling an exhilarating experience filled with a sense of aliveness. Webster's dictionary defines "excel" as "being distinguishable by superiority; to be more than or greater than; to surpass others, as in quality or quantity." This is *not* the sense in which I am using the word "excel" as applied to star-chasers.

My conception of a star-chaser is someone who goes all out, 100 percent, and is measured by his or her own internal standard of 100 percent. The dictionary definition of excel is the one I suspect we most commonly embrace in terms of pitted competition, where there are *winners* and *losers*. The necessity for these descriptions, regardless of who crossed the finish line first, is right back into survival – "the need to surpass others." To realize that it is necessary for someone to actually "*be*" a loser, before the winner can be a winner, is vitally important. In other words, the loser must actually acknowledge through communication having lost; if he doesn't, the situation was merely two individuals competitively participating in an activity.

Think about times when you participated in competitive activities in which there were agreed upon rules for winning and losing. In those cases where you gave 100 percent effort and didn't win, did you feel like a loser? Of course not. If the so-called loser does not declare having lost, then the winner has not won. From a survival standpoint, this declaration or acknowledgment is even more important to the winner than the competition or the prize.

To actually *realize* this point is tremendously empowering, since winning and losing are actually a function of one's ego, not one's self-worth or self-esteem. These can't be given or taken by deeds or by anyone. It's an illusion to believe that through success or nonsuccess, one's self-worth is increased or decreased; what is varied is one's ego, which "requires" winning to be "better than" something, someone, etc.

One may ask the question, "Why play the game if there are no winners and losers?" To which one reply is, "Is it more important to satisfy our egos through winning than it is to simply participate?" If ego satisfaction is more important, it is insightful to know and acknowledge that winning is a spiral without end and ultimately no sense of satisfaction. If satiating the ego through winning is the objective, it is probably one of those "cheeseless tunnels."

In my most recent experiences of participating in sports, professional competition, or other competitive activities, there is no doubt whatsoever when my effort is total. The ranking relative to someone or some others is absolutely immaterial! There is no sense of loss, gain, better, worse, superior, inferior, etc.; all of these have their ultimate genesis in survival, whereas, I have a sense of personal satisfaction. Even though I experience fear during the process (from my normal survival instincts), I am willing to risk anyway. Not allowing fear to be an insurmountable barrier is the part that really requires courage. Thus, I think of *courage as having fear and participating anyway* or simply *going beyond fear as a barrier.*

There is a distinction here again between the dictionary definition of courage and what I am expressing that is important. The dictionary, in part, defines "courage" as a "quality of being brave or fearless." I am not sure exactly what it means to be brave, but I know whenever I am courageous I am *also* fearful. However, after accomplishing something very scary for the first time, the fear is significantly lessened each succeeding time.

Probably one of the most common situations that raises the issue of fear for most of us is a career opportunity that shows up at the wrong time. If new opportunities did not show up when things were great, then there would be no risk and, hence, no fear. In my seminars I often present a situation where we are standing on the banks of the "stream of life." When an opportunity shows up, generally all we see is the first stone in the path to the other side. Most of us stand there waiting for the entire path of stones to appear before we are willing to step off. They never do, of course; and life is essentially about being a spectator. Star-chasers only need to see one stone to *go for it.* Somehow they have faith that the path of stones will appear *after* the commitment is made to step off, and it usually does.

> *"Whatever you can do, or dream you can, begin it.*
> *Boldness has genius, power, and magic in it."*
>
> *Goethe*

Finally, star-chasers tend to view life from two perspectives, *reasons* and *results.* The more results we produce, the less it is necessary to have reasons, and vice versa. The more our life is lived out of reasons, the greater the opportunity for us to engage those barriers that prevent us from producing the results we desire. Therefore, even adversity, arising from unique events in our lives, provides the possibility for us to transform misfortune into *opportunity.*

So Where's the Payoff, If Any?

Somewhere implied in all of what I have said so far, but not explicitly stated, is that reaching the goals or acquiring the symbols of success might not give us the sense of "making it" that we expected. At some point during the last five years of my life, I realized that reaching goals I had set for myself was not the source of ultimate satisfaction. I presently use a goal as a point or a marker along the path of life to provide direction and purpose for a particular activity and to acknowledge myself for the successful completion of a project. The goal, in itself, is not the source of ultimate satisfaction.

I have a sense that ultimate satisfaction must occur moment by moment, day by day, in the process of living itself. That is, satisfaction is not something we earn, but that which comes naturally to each of us as a result of our willingness to contribute to the well-being of those we live and work with.

So, ultimately, satisfaction is about contributing rather than receiving. Having the realization that life takes on a greater meaning through contribution was a long and difficult process for me. The key was not aiming at this realization as a goal, but the stepwise process of moving through the levels of responsibility discussed in Chapter 4.

What's Required to Be a "Star-Chaser"?

If star-chasing sounds like an exciting experiment, then the question of how to become a star-chaser naturally arises. The requirements are very simple. The willingness to systematically let go of the *sources* of our counterproductive behavior and to be courageous in the sense I have discussed above. That's it! I admit this is more easily said than done! Actually, the two are inextricably tied, since the moment we are confronted with the source of some counterproductive behavior, fear is the barrier.

What's convenient about the opportunity here is that we can go at our own pace. We're all climbing this "infinite mountain" that has no top with a sign labelled "You've made it!" However, the higher we climb, the greater the quality of life.

On Being Creative

The instant we let go of a counterproductive source of our well-being, growth, and productivity, a space is automatically created for something new to happen. This is the essence of the creative act. Thus, creativity comes from nothing and is manifested as something. Creativity is the opportunity for possibility, before definition, process, or form, and is outside of time. In retrospect, *creativity is bringing into being that which previously did not exist.* My perception is that we are not creative by simply thinking. Thinking involves the response of memory to what we already know. Thus, creativity is not solely the manipulation and change of existing facts, objects, ideas, and knowledge; and, as a result of the creative process, these also occur.

95

Being creative involves what I call step-function or nonlinear learning. It is a discontinuous jump above the base of knowledge and a reorientation in our way of seeing results. This concept is diagrammed in Figure 6 by the creation of a block above the foundation of present knowledge. As an example of this block, we might use the creation of the Theory of Relativity by Einstein or the unique music style created by Philip Glass. The dotted blocks represent the stepwise process that the scientific community used to ultimately prove the consistency of relativity with the base of knowledge in mathematics and physics. For Glass's music, whose roots lay in Eastern as well as Western music, the blocks represent the process of acceptance and acknowledgment of his talented works as a composer.

As a matter of fact, we are often creative, and we typically invalidate our creativity. The reason is that our creativity is normally not very high above the base, so the discontinuous jump is easily explained, in retrospect, by the dotted blocks. However, if we individually examine situations where we came up with a brilliant idea, painting, dish, novel, term paper, mechanical solution, experiment, etc., we tend to reduce its validity when the sensation is no longer there. This is so because we can't hold on to creativity, but we certainly have the opportunity to create again.

A question that may arise is, "How does our creativity differ from Einstein's and Glass's creativity?" There is no difference in creating, only in the manifested result. The flow is from the creation of possibility, to an experiential process, to a manifested result. With respect to individual abilities to create, there are no comparisons – creativity is creativity. In the realm of our total accumulated knowledge, there is "better than," based on an agreed system of values. Therefore, comparisons exist.

Einstein's and Glass's results, which are represented as objective knowledge by mathematical theory and music, were further removed above the base of knowledge and, therefore, required more proof in the sense of the dotted blocks before being accepted and acknowledged. It is important to recognize here that the ability to create at a given level above the base is directly proportional to the acquired knowledge in a given subject. Einstein was obviously extremely adept in physics and mathematics, and Glass in music.

We have all been creative at one time or another, some more often than others. The crucial question is, "How do we consistently and purposefully be creative?" This question was the objective for each student to uniquely discover in a course I recently presented. What we discovered was that there is no universal technique that consistently results in creative ideas or solutions. Each person has a unique process he or she goes through. We also discovered that we have difficulty in being purposefully creative because we are basically unaware, consciously, of the process we individually

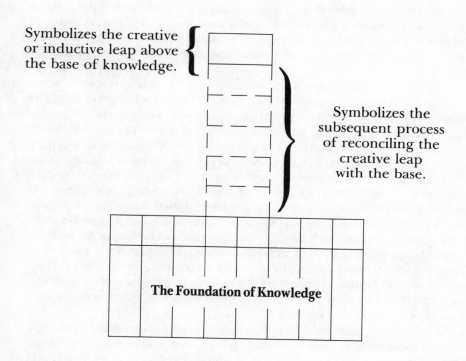

Symbolizes the creative or inductive leap above the base of knowledge.

Symbolizes the subsequent process of reconciling the creative leap with the base.

The Foundation of Knowledge

Figure 6 Illustration of the "inductive leap" above the base of knowledge which characterizes the creative process.

experience, and we tend to invalidate creative experiences that are subsequently easily explained.

Therefore, in order to gain some facility in each of our unique creative processes, we must begin with *increased awareness* and *acknowledgment* of ourselves. This process is most efficiently accomplished with a private diary having brief entries. However, it can also be accomplished by making regular mental notes.

Many of my professional responsibilities in teaching, research, seminars, and workshops involve creative presentations and approaches. The technique I personally use to initiate the process leading to the "inductive leap" is to first thoroughly inform myself of all the vitally important *and* relevant data, such as group size, logistics, attitudes, ideas, opinions, prejudices, interests, etc. From this point, the process becomes less definable, although I am consciously aware that it is occurring at an unconscious level. I essentially give myself conscious mental instructions to process the information I have fed into my mind (computer), based upon *specific requests* (this is important!) from me to come up with specific creative recommendations. I am also consciously alert to any information having to do with the subject being processed, such as books, newspapers, television, etc. I even notice myself steering informal conversations toward soliciting expert and layman advice. I am actively engaged and I can feel it moment by moment. Like clockwork, I always get my requests, usually during a morning shower, or while walking or driving alone.

The greatest difficulty I have in this process is that, quite often, the recommendations I receive are initially paradoxical and/or unconventional! This, of course, is what creativity is all about, the totally unexpected and certainly unconventional. On one occasion, I was instructed to present one of my workshops in the reverse order in which it made logical developmental sense. Who am I to stifle my creative recommendations! The presentation was a huge success.

On another occasion, I was invited to lead a workshop on communication from an organization that perceived there was a real difficulty in listening and understanding each other's point of view. My thoughts were that the session was, in large part, going to be about everyone justifying their point of view and in conclusion, having made no difference. The creative instructions I received were to *reframe* the session into one centered around the question, "How would you like your organization to function in the area of communication?" At the outset, we established specific goals based on the reframed question. Therefore, the seminar discussion was about what was required of each of them to achieve these goals and an in-depth look at their individual willingness to do so. This approach did make a difference to that group.

In order to creatively teach a course, I find that it is vital for me to discover what my student partners are interested in achieving and their level of commitment. I usually do so by having them respond to a one-page questionnaire *at the beginning* of the course, or, if the class is small enough, having a discussion. I always attempt to understand their objectives and get a clear understanding of what we are jointly committed to before getting into the content presentation. This is part of the data-gathering process I referred to earlier. Only after having accumulated all the necessary information and input am I in a position to construct a course that is uniquely designed for that particular group, without necessarily superimposing the memory of material or procedures that worked in previous courses.

Personal Freedom, an Essential Requirement for Creativity

Although I have not specifically mentioned it thus far, there is a fundamental requirement in being consistently and purposefully creative. That requirement is personal freedom. Without freedom there can be no creativity. Perhaps the most impacting aspect of freedom that I discovered is: my own personal freedom has nothing to do with my concepts or corresponding action in bringing it about. In fact, in the sense I am speaking of freedom, it has absolutely nothing to do with my opinions, ideas, feelings, beliefs, views, thoughts, impressions, ideals, or judgments about personal freedom. On the other hand, it has everything to do with simply being natural. *True freedom is letting go of the necessity of having attachments* – personal, professional, monetary, comfort, ideals, and objects, etc. Therefore, being free is not available to those of us who require conditions or attachments for being free. The freedom I am speaking of cannot be acquired or earned, it can only be created. In fact, the two are synonymous in a way; since we cannot create without freedom, the two are inextricably coupled.

The freedom necessary for creativity does not involve agreeing or disagreeing with someone else's concepts, ideas, or thoughts, but seeing together or individually how it really is without evaluation, judgment, or opinion. Until recently I had rarely experienced true freedom purposefully, primarily because I thought that it required my doing something to bring it about. I had always believed that personal freedom was an acquisition or something to work towards; a state of mind or a condition. I realize now that true freedom is always available and has always been available.

Freedom is not a "state of mind." A state of mind is a conceptually derived condition that dictates a way of acting; being natural requires no action.

Therefore, the freedoms of religion, voting, free movement, speech, lawful assembly, governmental choice, etc., are not what I am addressing

99

here. Those freedoms exist in another realm. I am also in no way making comparisons between those freedoms and the freedom I am discussing which is required for creativity. Those freedoms are for the most part conceptually derived and dictate a way of experiencing or acting.

Star-Chasing and Risking Are Really One and the Same

Somehow, the common theme that appears to run through every chapter of this book is the *willingness to risk*. Every chapter, in one way or another, has dealt with fear. Where there is fear, there is risk, whether real or imagined. The greater the opportunity, obviously, the greater the risk. Star-chasers are willing to risk. In fact, star-chasers view risk in a similar manner that, it is said, the Chinese view crises: by combining the symbols for the words "danger" and "opportunity." Therefore, risking is viewed as an opportunity.

The question of risk is certainly involved when we consider a change of jobs or profession. Sometimes the most difficult part of this process is moving to the place where we allow ourselves to consider other professional alternatives without limitations or conditions being involved. A situation that occurred in one of my workshops involved a successful professional women named Laurie, who had attended with the intent of discovering the source of her job dissatisfaction. During an in-depth exercise, the participants were asked to write, in detail, the description of their *ideal job* without any limitations or conditions attached. Laurie realized during the course of this exercise that everything she wanted, in terms of new responsibilities, could actually be achieved at her present place of work. The next week she rewrote her job description, presented it to her boss, who enthusiastically supported it, and within two weeks she essentially had a new job.

The important point to recognize is that when our present work is not as fulfilling as it may have been previously, it does not automatically mean we need to leave our present place of employment. The instant there are no conditions tied to our consideration, the possibilities are infinite, including leaving or remaining.

The willingness to risk is an issue that is very much part of a process occurring in my life at present. Although I am very securely established in my professional discipline and am a tenured university professor, I am naturally attracted to the activities discussed in this book. This process began several years ago when it was easy for me to either ignore consciously or simply deny this fact. I bring to it the same kind of boyish enthusiasm and naivete that I initially did in teaching. The fact is, I intend to pursue this activity full-time and stop pretending that it is a passing fancy or, at best, an avocation. Therefore, I have decided to take the risk.

Even writing this book, outside of the field I am professionally most comfortable in, is a risk for me. It is also an exciting opportunity and one which has totally consumed my day-to-day activities. I have been committed to it in the sense expressed in the prefatory statement to this chapter.

Therefore, reduced to its lowest common denominator, star-chasing is simply the same as risking; and, in the process, practically every subject we have discussed in this book comes up for consideration. The level of risking is totally a personal choice having no evaluation, judgment, or comparison. So you see, the truth is, we are all star-chasers, risking – out of choice – at the level that is both appropriate and comfortable.

"Sometimes it seems to me that in this
absurdly random life there is some inherent justice
in the outcome of personal relationships.
In the long run, we get no more
than we have been willing to risk giving."

Sheldon Kopp [7]

REFERENCES

1. J. Krishnamurti, *The Awakening of Intelligence*, A Discus Book, Avon Books, 1976.

2. Sir K. Popper, *In Pursuit of Truth;* The Nature of Knowledge, pg. 128.

3. C. R. Rogers, *A Way of Being*, Houghton Mifflin Company, 1980.

4. A. H. Maslow, *Toward a Psychology of Being*, Van Nostrand Reinhold Company, 1968.

5. J. Powell, S. J., *Unconditional Love*, Argus Communications, A Division of DLM, Inc., 1978.

6. H. Selye, *Stress Without Distress*, A Signet Book, New American Library, Inc., 1974.

7. S. Kopp, *If You Meet Buddha on the Road, Kill Him!*, Bantam Books, New York, 1972.

*"One can see that it is a waste of energy
to follow anybody, you understand?
To have a leader, to have a guru, because
when you follow you are imitating, you
are copying, you are obeying, you are
establishing authority. . . and so you are
comparing yourself with another, whether
'The Other' is a saint, a hero, a god,
an idea, or an ideology."*

J. Krishnamurti
The Awakening of Intelligence

*"While seeking to be taught the Truth, the
Disciple learns only that there is nothing
that anyone else can teach him. . . The
secret is that there is no secret."*

Sheldon Kopp
If You Meet the Buddha on the Road, Kill Him!

INNOVATIONS CONSULTING, INC.

Innovations Consulting, Inc. is a corporation which exists to provide programs for personal and organizational transformation.

The corporation is comprised of a Seminar Division, a Publishing Division, and a Media Division.

The programs of the Seminar Division which are uniquely designed for organizations, businesses, and corporations are:

- Insights for Success
- Diversity and the Empowered Organization
- Valuing and Managing Cultural Diversity in the Workplace
- Empowering the Work Force
- The Qualities of Leadership
- Creativity and Innovation

Other books and tapes available from the Publishing Division are:

Realizations, a two-cassette audio tape edition, which complements the book, with more than two and one-half hours of valuable discussion by the author, Dr. William A. Guillory.

$14.95

Rodney, by William A. Guillory, is the first in a series of transformational books for children. It is the story of a boy growing up in Kansas City, Missouri as he attempts to understand his relationships with his family, relatives, and friends. Each chapter provides an opportunity for meaningful discussions between parents and children which will lead to enhancement of their communication and relationship.
70 pages, spiral bound $6.95

Rodney Goes to the Country, by William A. Guillory, is the second book in the Rodney series which describes Rodney's experiences during a summer vacation spent with relatives in southern Louisiana on a farm. This book describes Rodney's learning of the world beyond his parents' home, that all young people can identify with, and the establishment of relationships with his extended family.
125 pages, spiral bound $7.95

It's All an Illusion, by William A. Guillory, is also available from Innovations. This is an entertaining story about a mysterious old man who engages a college student in a series of questions that ultimately involve the student's most fundamental beliefs, leading him to rather disturbing and exciting new insights that permanently change his life.

96 pages, paperback $6.95

If you wish to order any of these materials, or inquire into other information regarding the seminars, workshops, or one-on-one offerings, please write or call:

Innovations Consulting, Inc.
488 East 6400 South
Suite 475
Salt Lake City, Utah 84107
(801) 268-3313